TRAINING

THE

Two-Year-Old

COLT

Cover Photo: Author Laurie Truskauskas with San Leo Scarlet, alias "T.C."

Endsheets: A view of the Silver Creek Farm training center.

Back Cover: The author, Laurie Truskauskas.

TRAINING
THE
Two-Year-Old
COLT

Laurie Truskauskas

Photography by Bob Porzio

Alpine
PUBLICATIONS
Loveland, Colorado

TRAINING THE TWO-YEAR-OLD COLT

Copyright © 1998 by Laurie Truskauskas

ISBN 1-57779-004-9

Library of Congress Cataloging-in-Publication Data
Truskauskas, Laurie, 1957-
      Training the two-year-old colt / Laurie Truskauskas ;
photography by Bob Porzio.
            p.   cm.
      Includes index.
      ISBN 1-57779-004-9
      1. Horses--Training.   I. Title.
      SF287.T75   1998
636.1'3--dc21   97-43429
                                                              CIP

Many manufacturers secure trademark rights for their products. When Alpine Publications is aware of a trademark claim, we print the product name in initial capital letters.

Alpine Publications accepts no responsibility for medical information, suggested treatments or recommended vaccinations mentioned herein. The reader is advised to check with a local, licensed veterinarian before giving medical attention.

Photography by Bob Porzio
Photography for Chapter 2 by Marianne Pirotta
Cover and text design by Dianne Nelson, Shadow Canyon Graphics

1 2 3 4 5 6 7 8 9 0
Printed in the United States of America

C O N T E N T S

This book is dedicated to Joe Ferro

of Grand View Ranch, Harwinton, Connecticut.

While I worked with him, he taught me

a "little bit" about breeding, training, and evaluating

a horse properly.

FOREWORD

I have been involved with the Quarter Horse Association since its inception in 1942 and incorporated many of the original rules and regulations. I started working with horses many years before that, starting with my father's hack stable in the 1920s. Then I advanced to showing gaited horses, learning from some of the best men in the country.

With my many years in the horse business, I have seen many of the great horses and I've been good friends with many great trainers over the years. Quite a few of them lived or worked here at Grand View Ranch at one time or another.

I've worked with many types of horses, but over the years gained the most appreciation for the Quarter Horse breed. At Grand View Ranch, located in Harwinton, Connecticut, where Laurie Truskauskas has worked off and on over the years with both myself and my son, Roy Ferro, we have bred and trained World Champion Reining horses, Western Pleasure horses, Halter horses, and Hunter Under Saddle horses.

Reining horses are the top of the line Western Horses, performing lead changes, sliding stops, spins and roll backs. It takes a special kind of horse with the right kind of mind and the conformation and the athletic ability to hold up to the demands of this sport, and I pride myself on raising those types of horses.

Working with Laurie has been a pleasure, and I have enjoyed being able to pass on the knowledge that I've gained over the years to someone so interested and quick to learn. She is as capable as anyone I've ever had the pleasure to help, and more so than many of them, with an intense desire to learn about all aspects of training and breeding.

With the variety of activity here at the farm, she has been able to learn and succeed at breeding, teasing, foaling, as well as starting the two–year–olds either for reining or for over–fence work, and how to evaluate a horse correctly and honestly. A horse with a good mind is my goal in breeding, and one that I've tried to emphasize to many people over the years.

Joe Ferro
Grand View Ranch
Harwinton, Connecticut

ACKNOWLEDGEMENTS

I would like to thank the following people:

My Mom, Bernice Bunn, for buying me that very first pony, helping me throughout the years, and doing the last check on this book for errors.

My "ex" mother-in-law, Lucy Truskauskas, for telling me to write a book after she read one of my letters.

My sons, Don and Jon, and grandson Michael, for keeping my life so interesting.

Bob Porzio of Atlantic Photography, Glastonbury, Connecticut who took the photos for this book and spent the time cropping and developing each one to perfection.

Joe Ferro, who taught me much of what I know and who gave me the courage and confidence to put it all on paper.

Betty McKinney, the publisher at Alpine Publications, who accepted this book, and the Alpine staff; all of whom have been helpful and who will put these pages into book form. (Thanks!)

And thanks to the editors at various magazines, most importantly, Jack Lewis and June Carlier of *Horse and Horseman* magazine. They accepted the first article that I ever wrote and ran a ten-month series shortly after that. I also thank Bonnie Ebsen Jackson, *The Western Horse*, Pat Close, *The Western Horseman*, Christy Dement, *The Quarter Horse Journal*, Ellen Gelting, *Hoof Print*, Bill Brassard, *Horses Monthly*, and all of the other editors who have complimented my writing and gave me the confidence to write this book.

And final thanks to all of the horses that I've owned or trained. I learn just a little bit more from each one of them.

The outside of a horse is good

for the inside of a man (or woman).

CHAPTER ONE

Thinking Like a Horse: The Basics of Training

———— ◆ ————

Is there a well-kept secret to training a horse? Throughout this book, I stress the importance of consistency, timing, repetition, feel, and fairness. These are the key ingredients required to train a horse. Think about what you are telling your horse with each and every cue that you give, and how a colt or horse *may interpret those same cues.* Each cue that you use should tell a horse something. It should not be meaningless garble or be conflicting to him.

The day that training became easy for me was when I learned to "think like a horse"—to talk to a horse in a language that he could understand. I learned to speak *only* when I had *something to say* to him. The rest of the time, I left him alone and did nothing.

GIVE CONSISTENT AIDS

For a horse to learn the proper or required response to a given cue or signal, that cue must be given in a consistent manner. It must be "told" to the horse the same exact way, each and every time it is given. Imagine that someone tells you to walk on one day, to perambulate on the next day, to promenade on the following day, to saunter next week, and finally to traverse. Would you understand which is the right thing to do? (I wouldn't.) A horse feels the same way.

1

Each cue that you give to a horse must mean the same thing every time that it is given, and for this to occur, it must be given in the same way. By giving consistent cues, a horse will, in time, understand what the cue means. You must consistently reward the horse for responding correctly (by release of pressure) so that he will understand that he has performed the correct response to your cue and that he will be rewarded for doing so. The cue may be exaggerated in the beginning to show a horse the proper response to a specific cue or signal, but the cue itself must remain consistent.

Consistent use of an aid can teach a horse that while leg pressure used in one way may mean to move forward, leg pressure used in another way may mean to move sideways or laterally away from leg pressure. Both cues are given by leg pressure, but each cue is given in a different manner and therefore means a different thing.

Left: Cues may be exaggerated initially to show a colt what you want. Correct equitation applies more after a colt is trained. Here, I've used my inside (left) leg and inside rein to ask the colt to move to the right. Right: As soon as he responds by taking the cross-over step, I release all pressure to reward him.

USING THE AIDS IMPROPERLY

Using aids that are inconsistent or not clearly defined will only confuse a horse. For example, if you've taught your horse to bend around your inside calf while turning in a small circle, and to move away from heel pressure, then you'll only confuse him if you try to use your heel to make him bend around your leg in a small circle.

The horse would be correct to move his hip, if not his entire body, laterally or sideways to the outside, enlarging the circle, rather than bending around your leg to make a small circle. Punishing a horse for such a response is not fair to him because the mistake was caused by rider error and the use of inconsistent aids. The horse interpreted your cue to mean one thing because that is what he was taught, and so he performed what he thought was the correct response.

Along the same line, if you always shorten your reins before preparing to lope, a horse will soon interpret that as the cue to lope, rather than waiting for your leg cue to lope. The horse thinks that if he lopes from your shortening of the reins, he can avoid the leg-pressure cue. And while we use this same process to train a horse, beware of habits such as this that you may have fallen into. The horse is trying to please—trying to respond to the lightest possible signal. To effectively train a horse, you must be aware first of all that you have given a cue, and secondly, you need to understand what those cues are telling the horse at all times.

TIME YOUR CORRECTIONS

Timing plays an extremely important role in training. For a horse to understand that he is being corrected, you must correct him within three seconds. Waiting longer than three seconds will leave him confused, and he will have no idea why he is being corrected. He'll have no way of associating the punishment with the crime. Not only will he not understand the punishment, he'll become resentful because he was punished unfairly. Jerking on a horse's mouth because you are angry is the most unfairly used correction that I see. Often, this happens minutes after a horse misbehaved, leaving the horse totally confused, with a sore mouth, and having no idea how to avoid that same unfair correction the next time. Is it no wonder that some horses resort to bad behavior?

For example, if a horse runs out of a gate, and you dismount, bring him back to the barn, and then hit him, he will be utterly confused as to why you are punishing him—and rightly so. Dismounting and putting a horse back in his stall makes a horse feel that he is being rewarded. A horse will then try to repeat the same behavior that caused him to get rewarded. The next time he walks by an open gate, he will try to go out of it to get his reward of stall rest again.

Taking a horse to a stall and then punishing him after that much time has elapsed, as well as rewarding him by dismounting, will leave a horse thinking that you are not to be trusted. A horse will feel that he has done nothing wrong and that you are beating him for the pure joy of being a bully. You will never gain his trust or respect, and without trust and respect, you will never be able to train a horse properly.

To effectively correct a horse for running out of the gate, you must immediately, *as soon as he begins to run out of the gate* (not ten steps after he is out of the gate), correct him. I correct a horse in this situation by pulling him into three or four tight circles. Circling is uncomfortable for a horse and he will learn to avoid the behavior that causes him to get pulled into a tight circle. To make circling a harsher correction (perhaps on a horse that has tried to run out of a gate many times before), bump the horse hard with your outside heel as you pull him into tight circles. Pulling a horse in a tight circle is acceptable if you first gain contact with his mouth and pull him around. Snatching at his mouth or jerking on the reins is not acceptable under any circumstance. Use those three seconds to gently gain contact with the horse's mouth, then pull, not jerk, the horse around in tight circles. Lock your hand on your hip if you have a strong horse. Force him into small circles to show him that it is more uncomfortable to make those small circles than it is to rush out of a gate.

Then, so that the horse truly understands the correction, ask him to walk past the gate a second time. If he tries to bolt out again, repeat the circling correction. After correcting him, walk by the gate a third, fourth, or fifth time, repeating the correction as needed, until finally the horse walks past the gate without bolting out of it. When he finally walks past a gate correctly, remain relaxed to tell him that he is correct.

If a colt tries to bite you, and you do not immediately punish him, within three seconds, the colt will not associate the punishment with the crime. The same is true if a colt kicks at you. One strong correction is often all that it takes to tell a colt biting and kicking are unacceptable. But you must time the correction to occur *as soon as* he tries to bite or kick. Waiting longer than three seconds will only confuse him. After three seconds, he will have already forgotten what he did wrong and will think that you are correcting him for something totally unrelated.

RELEASE PRESSURE

The release of pressure is as important as timing your corrections. The release of pressure is often the only way that you have to reward a horse. You must be able to feel that the horse has

To teach a horse to turn, you must release the pressure as soon as he does turn.

responded correctly, then immediately release all pressure—this is proper timing. If you pull on the reins to make a horse stop and do not immediately release your rein pressure to reward a horse for stopping, why should he stop the next time?

SIGNAL LIGHTLY

If you lightly pick up your reins as a way to signal your colt to stop, and you do not release your rein pressure as soon as the colt does stop, why should he stop the next time? If you don't release pressure as soon as the colt stops, you are sending a conflicting message—stop and what? You are asking the colt to stop on a light signal, but you are not rewarding him for stopping. How is he to understand the proper response? How is he to understand what you are saying to him?—to stop and wait and to relax until you tell him to do something else. And finally, why should he stop on a light signal the next time if you continue to pull anyway? A colt will try to comprehend what you are asking of him by interpreting the additional pressure. My reiners would immediately begin to back up if I continued to hold contact on the reins after they stopped. I always release pressure on the reins after a horse stops to reward him before I pick up contact again to ask the horse to back up.

If you release all pressure when the colt does stop, it says to the colt, "Yes—thank you for stopping as I asked, for obeying my signal. If you stop that way every time that I ask, I will always ask you to stop on a light signal (freeing you from the pressure on your mouth), and I will always reward you by immediate release of pressure."

If you initially ask your colt to move away from leg pressure, and he takes one step away from your leg or your spur, you must immediately (in the initial stages of training) release leg pressure to tell the colt that he is correct. After a couple of days, when he understands to take one step away from pressure, knowing that he will get rewarded for doing so, then you may ask him to take two steps. You must still reward him for those two steps—by release of pressure—as soon as he takes those two steps. The next day or next week, you may ask for three steps, then four, and so on. Think like a horse and think about how the horse interprets your cues.

REPEAT, REPEAT, REPEAT

Through the repetition of your cues, rewards, and corrections, you can show a horse what is acceptable behavior and what is not. If a horse learns that he will consistently get punished (small circle) as soon as he tries to run out a gate, and is consistently rewarded (through the relaxed feel of your body and the absence of cues) every time he goes properly past the gate, the horse will learn what you expect of him. Sometimes a horse learns this quickly, and sometimes you must repeat the same correction/reward over and over again. You may feel as if the horse will never understand what you are trying to "say" to him. Rest assured, that with enough repetition, almost any behavior can be learned or unlearned.

TREAT HIM FAIRLY

A horse must be treated fairly. You must ask or tell a horse to perform using the appropriate set of cues so that the horse may respond. Your corrections to a horse must be appropriate to the level of his disobedience. A horse that bites or kicks should be punished immediately and as severely as you are capable of (within reason, of course). Punishing a horse severely on the first offense will often stop the behavior permanently. Picking or nagging at a horse in such a case will often make him think that it is a game, and he'll continue the behavior as long as it is fun for him.

Punishing a colt by whipping or spurring him when you ask him to perform a walk-to-lope departure the first time you ride that colt is unfair. He will become frightened because he will not understand why he is being punished. He will be confused by your signals and afraid to try at all. Some colts will just stop and stand and "take" the beating, yet it will in no way tell them what they are being punished for. Others will bolt out of fear, still not understanding the correction.

The colt learns that he responded correctly to my loping cue because I let him lope on a loose rein.

If you go to a slightly stronger cue than the original light-heel cue, for example, bumping the colt until he lopes, that is an appropriate stronger cue and a horse will accept it as such. Adding a tap from a crop is the next strongest cue. But to go directly to whipping a colt for not loping from a walk is unfair to him and is not a suitable punishment. The colt will begin to resent you and will never put his heart into his work, and you will end up with a balky, confused colt.

After a colt begins to understand what is acceptable and what he will be corrected for, he will flick an ear back and forth or point one ear toward the direction in which he will move. Walk or jog past an open gate in an arena and you'll see a colt flick his ear to the right before he tries to head out the gate. The colt knows that it is wrong and is waiting to see if the rider on his back is paying attention. If the rider is "sleeping," the colt thinks that it is acceptable to choose his own path, or at least try to choose his own path, usually out the gate and back to the barn. The flicking of an ear is a signal to you to give the colt a light squeeze from both calves to send him forward or perhaps to give him an additional rein cue to stay straight past the gate.

If you grab the reins and yank the colt around in a tight circle when the colt is only flicking his ears back and forth (the colt is questioning you—is it all right for him to go out the open gate?), you are being unfair if you punish him harshly. A colt questioning you in such a way requires a soft answer from you. Using reins or legs to direct him past the gate, keeping his mind on the job at hand, is acceptable—yanking him around is not. However, if the colt bolts out the gate, you are correct in pulling him in three to four tight circles to show him that it is in his best interest to stay on the rail and go past the gate. After the tight circles, you must then immediately reenter the ring and make the colt walk past the gate correctly. If he misbehaves, correct him again and again. Stay with it until the colt gives in.

Most colts will not resent such a correction, because they know that they are wrong and are trying to get away with it. This is similar to a child who tries to take a piece of candy right before dinner. He knows that he shouldn't but tries anyway. If you scold the child, he'll accept it. However, if you scold a child because he is standing next to the candy (but has no desire to take a piece because he knows that you'll be angry), he'll get resentful because you *thought* that he might take a piece.

MAKE HIM RESPECT YOU

A colt must respect you before he will try to learn. If he thinks that he is the "top dog," he will try to get his own way rather than be respectful of what you are telling him. A colt must respect you to learn. Spoiled colts are the hardest to train. We'd all love to love our horses, but just like children, they must be taught respect and to learn their place in society. Don't be afraid "to get after" a colt. Respect can be gained without abusing a colt in any way.

Be sure that you can read when the colt has given in so that you can stop the punishment. Never use *any* type of punishment without knowing exactly why you are correcting a colt. Never punish a colt because you are having a bad day. A punishment is only permissible when the colt has performed in such a way that he must be told that what he has done is unacceptable. The punishment must fit the crime.

If a colt tries to walk over or through you and push you out of his way, you are more than justified in taking a bat (crop) to his chest and giving him a hard crack. If he tries to rear and strike at you with his front leg, as some stud colts are prone to try once or twice, you are justified in shanking him back twenty or thirty feet (staying to the side so that he can't get you with a front hoof if he decides to go up again). Your safety is of the utmost importance—never forget that.

On the same note, don't look to punishment as the answer to everything that a colt may do wrong. Often you tell a colt more by a reward, such as the release of pressure (which tells a colt that he has performed satisfactorily). Releasing rein pressure as soon as a colt stops is an extremely important reward, asking him to move away from your leg for a step or two and then removing your leg so that he may walk straight forward is another reward.

A relaxing walk around the pen also helps to tell a colt that he responded correctly.

Don't pat your colt on the neck for every good step that he makes. He'll come to expect those pats and will not move without them. Release of pressure (or of the cue) or a relaxing walk around the ring on a loose rein will tell your colt that you are pleased. Save the pats on the neck for the really big breakthroughs.

REINFORCE YOUR CORRECTIONS AND REWARDS

Using a correction or reward consistently is as important as using the aids consistently. If you allow a colt to goof off one day and don't bother to correct him for the same mistake that you corrected him for yesterday, he will become confused. He'll have no idea if today he'll get corrected and therefore he should behave, or if he can goof off and get away with it. When a colt is trained inconsistently, he'll always test to see what kind of day it is. A colt likes structure in his life. He is happiest when he knows exactly what the rules are and the same rules *must apply every day.*

While this may become monotonous to you, this is the way it must be. The glamour comes after a colt is trained—then you can show the world what you've accomplished. You must continue to reinforce that correct behavior is just that—correct behavior. Anything else will not be tolerated. A colt may test you, but if you train solidly, you should be able to work through whatever problems may arise. Your colt will understand that he will get corrected by a stronger leg cue if he tries to jog into the lope, and if he fails to respond to the leg cue, he will get tapped with a crop. If he tries to run out of a gate, he will understand that a correction will follow. He must learn that it is in his best interest to respond properly and correctly as soon as possible after you ask.

Horses are very simple creatures to figure out if you put the time into reading what your colt is telling you. You must apply your aids, corrections, and rewards in the proper manner every time so that a colt can learn to understand what you are "saying." While you are training a colt, you'll see him perform the correct response and flick his ears, waiting to see if he gets praised by you or gets the reward of release of pressure. Most horses sincerely want to please, although on occasion you may first have to show a colt that it is in his best interest to learn.

REWARD BY A REST

Standing and letting a colt rest can be used as a big reward if it is timed correctly. Let's use an example of a colt that hesitated to go over a pole on the ground. He finally lets you convince him that it is safe to cross over. He walks over it three or four more times. If you let him stand and rest immediately— say ten feet after the pole—this is a reward that a colt can understand. He walks properly over the pole, and you tell him that this is what you wanted by letting him rest and leaving him alone as he enjoy his rest. To reward a colt in this way, sit so that your body is relaxed, telling the colt through your body language that he may relax.

If you walk over the jump a few times, then walk all over the arena for another three to four minutes, and *then* let the colt stop and rest, the reward is not as effective. While a colt will still benefit somewhat by a relaxing walk around the arena, after being shown that he must cross the jump, it is more effective to let him rest *immediately* after he crosses over it because it is in a language that he can more easily understand during the initial training.

Don't misunderstand what I'm saying. All colts should obey orders to go forward on command. Save this type of rest and reward for when the colt has shown you that he is really afraid of a particular obstacle or for those times when you are working on a new maneuver and he makes a big breakthrough. I only use this type of reward on occasion. After a colt crosses an obstacle a few times or for a few days, a brief walk on a loose rein after completing the entire series of maneuvers is all that is required if you feel that he deserves a reward. Some beginning trainers feel that they must reward a colt for each tiny maneuver, but this only teaches the colt to wait for his pat on the neck or his reward of a rest for each small accomplishment. Don't carry your rewards to this extreme. A release of pressure at the proper time is effective in most cases.

REWARD BY UNTACKING

Dismounting and untacking a horse can be used as a big reward—again, if used properly. I try to complete a new maneuver or work on a troublesome exercise at the end of my lesson. As soon as I feel that the colt has shown a slight improvement or understanding of the new maneuver, I will dismount and loosen the saddle right there to reward him for trying. The colt will think, "Gee—if I do it right, she gets off my back and puts me away. I'll try harder the next time and maybe she'll get off sooner."

To teach your horse to flex, take hold of his mouth and ask him to give.

When he gives, reward him by releasing pressure.

REMEMBER—TIMING AND FEEL

Timing and feel are training methods that I try to stress to all of my students. Before you use an aid, think of how the horse might interpret it.

After enough fair, consistent, properly timed repetitions of the same reward or correction, a colt will stop trying to do the things that he knows he will get corrected for and will try to do those things that he gets rewarded for. And that is what training is all about. That is how a colt learns.

TRAINING RULES TO POST IN YOUR BARN

Here are a few rules to keep in mind when training—not only when you start a colt under saddle, but whenever you work with any horse.

1. Every move that you make tells a horse something.
2. The release of pressure is a reward to a horse.
3. The absence of a cue or correction tells a horse that he is performing acceptably.
4. When your horse is performing acceptably, leave him alone—do nothing.
5. Correct a horse and then forget about it. Don't nag a horse.
6. You have three seconds to correct/reward a horse or he won't understand it.
7. A horse learns through the use of consistent, repetitious aids.
8. Many mistakes are caused by rider error. Many errors are wrongly blamed on the horse. Be sure to place the blame where it belongs.
9. Train your colt following a logical succession of steps, and build on each previously taught step. Allow your colt time to understand and interpret each cue or command and time to perform it, then reward him promptly for each correctly interpreted or performed maneuver.

Laying the Groundwork: Before You Begin Training the Two-Year-Old Colt

◆

IMPRINTING THE NEWBORN FOAL

Imprinting is the art of impressing your training methods upon a newborn foal. Using this method, a foal learns right from birth how to be led, tied, and to pick up his feet as his dam watches from the sidelines. This allows the foal to become comfortable with a human handler and he learns to accept various forms of equipment, the most basic being the halter and lead line. A foal also can be taught to accept clippers, fly spray bottles, traffic noises, or any number of other items to which you expose him. The time and training that you spend with your foal now will benefit him for years to come, most notably when you begin to prepare your two-year-old for work under saddle and that all-important first ride.

Imprinting as a method of training was first introduced and named by Robert Miller, DVM, but the actual method may vary from trainer to trainer. The important point to remember is that early training can only benefit a foal later in life, as long you perform it correctly. Do not scare a foal or teach him bad habits now because they will stay with him perhaps more easily than the good training habits that you wish to instill. Leaving a foal with bad habits or fear of certain articles can interfere with the entire training procedure as he becomes of saddle- breaking age.

Imprint training teaches a foal much that he will need to know later in life. In the first day or two of his life, he will learn to respect his dam as well as his human handler. In a matter of two to three hours, spread over the first few days, you can teach your foal to lead, tie, back, pick up his feet, and accept clippers. But you must remember that a foal has a limited attention span. Break down your lessons into small segments, and build each new maneuver on the previously taught maneuver. For example, you wouldn't expect a foal to tie before you first taught him to accept wearing a halter and to respect the lead rope. Plan your lessons accordingly. Ten to fifteen minutes at a time, three or four times a day, should suffice.

If you bring your mare in to foal in a large, clean, well–bedded (I prefer straw) stall, rather than let her foal outside in a pasture, you'll be better able to tell when her time is at hand and therefore have the opportunity to imprint the newborn. I spend ten to fourteen days with a newborn foal implementing my imprinting method. Then I turn him out until he is a yearling. Aside from routine shots and wormings, my work is done. I can walk up to him at any time. He is halter–broken in case of an emergency. He can be led beside his dam from pasture to pasture, or from pasture to barn. He remains calm and is easy to handle. Saddle breaking and future training are easier because the baby respects humans yet has very little fear of them or of the various types of equipment.

Birth

Once the mare foals, begin your imprint training as soon as possible. If you are present at the actual birth, you can towel dry your foal. This prevents the foal from getting a chill, and by

Get your foal used to having your hands all over his body.

rubbing the towel and your hands all over his body, you accomplish the first step in imprinting—getting your foal used to having your hands all over his body. Do it with enough pressure so that he feels you rubbing. The foal needs to feel the calm assurance that all is well.

Touch Your Foal

After your baby is dry and he accepts being touched with a towel, take hold of one ear and gently rub the outside. Repeat on the other side. Put your fingers inside, but not into the ear

Gently rub the foal's ears.

canal. Rub between his ears and down his face. Put your fingers in his nostrils, then into his mouth to rub his gums. Rub where the bit will later lie when he is of an acceptable age. Rub under his chin. Rub his face and up and down his neck. Do this until he accepts your hands all over his body. Rub between his legs and down his legs, and hold his hoofs. Run your hand down his back legs, under his tail, and under his belly. Rub behind his front legs, where your girth will go.

The sooner you start this, the easier it will be. If the baby resists, now is the time to teach him that his life will be much more comfortable if he gives in. If he learns as a foal that he can resist, think of how he will act when you begin to saddle break him. Teach him right from wrong now, and your job will be much easier later.

Rub the foal's gums to prepare him to open his mouth when the time comes to carry a bit.

Use some horse sense while you imprint the foal. A two-day-old foal is powerful enough to hurt you if he catches you off guard. If you start imprinting immediately at birth, the foal will not have much strength and will be more accepting. But do not feel that because you miss the first day, you should not go ahead and imprint your baby. Start this training at the first possible time. Just keep in mind that this is a 100-pound foal. Use horse sense as you would working around any horse.

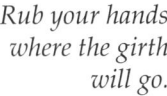

Rub your hands where the girth will go.

Halter Breaking

Have a small halter that will fit your foal and start halter breaking in the stall. After putting on the halter and adjusting it for a correct fit, cluck to tell the foal that you want him move forward. Then gently tug on the halter and ask him to turn toward you. Always cluck first. Cluck first to ask, then tug to tell. Push his hind end forward to enforce your command.

Don't ask for a tight circle initially because the colt may fall. Ask for forward motion. The little bit of a circle makes it easier for you to get your arm around his rump to push him forward the first time or two. Every time you stop, say "Whoa!" Whoa means stop-freeze-don't move. If you say "Whoa!" and he doesn't freeze, a light snap on the lead rope reinforces that whoa means whoa. As he stops, scratch his neck to let him know that he is correct. The foal will come to look for the reward. A scratch, as well as your tone of voice, lets the baby know that he has done what you've asked.

Eventually, ask the foal to move straight forward, instead of moving in circles. After a couple of days, a rump rope used once or twice (explained in more detail later in this chapter), will help to enforce to the foal that he must obey your go-forward command. Again, cluck first, followed by a light tug on the halter. If he hasn't moved, a quick tug on the rump rope will bring him forward.

Every time you stop, say "Whoa!" Consistency—the same cues in the same order, every time—is how horses learn. Be fair to your horse. Be consistent in your cues, and do not confuse your horse.

As the foal accepts forward motion, go back to your circles. Place one hand on your lead rope and the other where your leg will be. Use that hand to gently push him out, away from pressure, for one or two steps. When you start to ride this colt, he'll easily learn to move away from leg pressure. Be sure to spend equal time on both sides, or more time on the side on which the colt gives you the most trouble.

Picking Up His Hooves

As the foal gets steady on his feet, run your hand down his legs. Say, "Pick it up" (or whatever your choice of words may be), and gently pick up his foot. Hold it for a second. Then put it down and scratch his neck or rump to let him know that he gave the desired response. Then pick it up again. Use the same cues, the same way, in the same order, every time. Do this three times per foot. After a few days, he will start to know what you want when you run your hands down his legs and say the words.

Always end on the best note possible, governed by the colt's previous actions. If necessary, return to something that he does well so that you may praise him for good behavior. Give him time to absorb what you are asking. If you have a problem with some part of your training with a foal, come back an hour later, and ask again. A foal has a short attention span and if you ask for too much, for too long a time period, he'll get resentful and will not learn. Break your lessons down into short segments.

Out of the Stall

Once the foal has accepted your stall lessons, leading him outside the stall is just one more step in the program. Lead the foal to the turnout pen, but before turning him loose, spend a few more minutes picking up his feet and rubbing his entire body. You may teach him to back by pushing on his chest for one or two steps as you ask him to back with the lead rope.

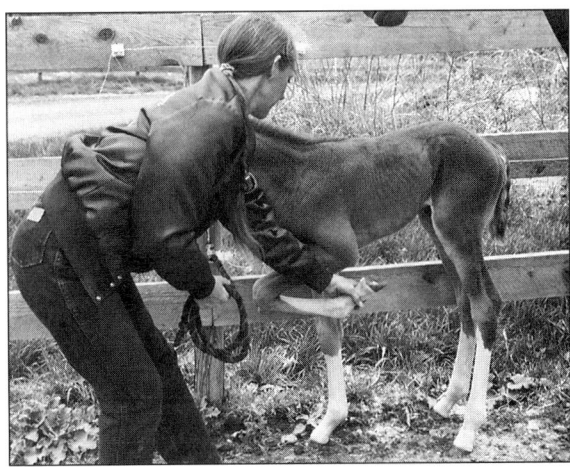

Teach the foal to pick up his feet now.

If a foal ever starts to rush forward past you as you are leading him, snap him back. You must be careful doing this, however. You don't want him to fall and hurt himself, yet he must learn that rushing is not acceptable. Use enough pressure to get your point across.

By the third day, your foal should be halter broken. It's not at all traumatic for him as it is if you let him grow up wild in a pasture and then take him away from his mother, and halter break him at six months of age.

Tying

You can teach a colt to stand tied by holding your rope and not moving. He won't be strong enough to pull you—yet. Or you may wrap the rope once around a pole and hold the other end. This way, he is not tied to a solid object, where there is a chance of injury. He probably will walk back, hit the end of the rope, and come forward. That is all there is to teaching him to tie. That is one of the benefits of imprinting.

An older horse that has never been tied before will obviously be upset over having his head tied to a pole or rail. He will fight for however long it takes to accept that he is tied and cannot move. He may paw, rear, pull back, and possibly throw himself on the ground. You can avoid all of this with imprint training, in which a foal enters life having respect for humans and a rope.

Now that he is halter broken, on your second or third day, lead him into stalls, barns, in your trailer (this is easier if it has a ramp), a chute (if you have one available), or anywhere that you want him to become accustomed to at a later date.

Take out your clippers and run them around his face, ears, and legs, but be careful because his skin will burn if the clippers are hot. Lay a saddle pad over his back so that he feels it there. Put your hands around his girth to prepare him for a saddle. Stand behind him but to the side, close enough so that if he kicks, he has no leverage and can't hurt you. Rub your hands on both sides of him at the same time. This will get him used to seeing shadows over his back and he won't spook as badly, if at all, when you mount for the first time.

These imprinted foals look to you for guidance and confidence. They're safer to work around, accept the training procedure with less stress, and wean more easily.

Remember that the cute little one-day-old baby will grow to be a 600- to 700-pound yearling. A horse or yearling that thinks he is a pet is not a pleasure to train.

You may have to restrain an untrained foal in this manner, but not an imprinted baby. Look at Splash's relaxed manner and closed eyes, showing that she is not afraid of people.

Respect

As you are imprinting your foal, he will have very little fear of you, so you must teach him respect. If he tries to bite you, "growl" at him in a rough tone of voice to let him know that biting is unacceptable behavior. If he tries it again, slap him, once, very hard on the neck, as you would an older horse. Be fair to him. Teach him right from the beginning that biting is not acceptable. Don't let him bite now or he will bite when he is older. Don't push him away, because then it becomes a game. If your voice command doesn't work the first time, one good, hard slap lets him know in no uncertain terms that biting is not acceptable.

If you are in the turnout area with your foal and he runs up to you and rears, use the sharp verbal "Hey" and wave your arms to scare him back so that he knows that rearing is not acceptable. Do not run and teach the foal to chase you. This may be cute when the foal is small but it is *not* cute when a 1,000-pound horse tries to run you down. Teach the foal that you *demand respect*. You are not a playmate and it is dangerous for him to think so. A baby can be spoiled easily by a well–intentioned owner, then he has to be sent off to a trainer to try to undo the damage that was done long before anyone sat on his back.

One hard slap, or correction, is more effective and humane in any training situation. Little taps will not impress a foal. Let your foal know from day one that unacceptable behavior is just that—not acceptable.

Weaning

Weaning is much less traumatic after imprint training. The foal can be led to the stall because he already knows a stall and the human handler from his experience after birth. It is not nearly as traumatic as getting hazed or chased into a stall for the first time and having the door slammed in his face. After he stays in for a few days, you can then turn him out to a different paddock with his buddies or pasture mates.

Letting Him Grow

Then turn him out to grow for a year. The ideal situation is to put a youngster in a large, safe pasture and let him learn to be a horse. Let him learn how to negotiate hills and banks, and to grow and develop his muscles. Bringing the colt in from time to time for a brief refresher course will keep these early lessons ingrained in his mind. You can feel confident that if you have done your work well, you will have a yearling that is halter broken and that will tie. He will pick up his feet and whatever else you may have taught him with a minimum of fuss.

You will have spent approximately two to three hours and you will have saved yourself months. You have avoided any stress to your foal and should now have a yearling who's ready to learn.

BASIC HANDLING FOR THE YOUNG COLT

If you missed imprinting your foal, or perhaps you bought a weanling that was not yet trained, you can still lay groundwork that will later help your colt with work under saddle. Every colt must be taught basic training and manners, as well as respect for a human handler. This basic training should include, at the very minimum, leading, tying, standing for grooming, and picking up his feet. By training a foal and then keeping these lessons ingrained in his mind through brief reschooling lessons until he is old enough to saddle break, you will also be prepared to treat your foal in an emergency and will have an enjoyable youngster to handle on a day-to-day basis. Saddle breaking will be easier, because your colt will trust and respect you.

Generally, the younger you start to handle your foal, the easier it will be. He will have less strength to fight you and will be more accepting of new procedures.

Keep Your Lessons Short

Training a foal doesn't require a long training session; in fact, it is quite the opposite. You must keep your lessons short because of a foal's attention span. You can work your foal ten to twenty minutes at a time, returning an hour or two later if you have a problem or if you want to be sure that this lesson is firmly ingrained in his mind. Forcing a foal to stay focused on you any longer than this is likely to cause problems. The foal will become resentful and may begin to fight you, putting you in the position of having to win the battle or risk letting him get away with something that could be the start of a bad habit. Avoid this possibility by keeping your lessons short. Break each lesson into small segments; then build on each previously learned step. Always end your lesson on a good note.

With a weanling that has not had much handling, you must also help him to overcome his initial fear of people as you teach him basic manners. Even if a colt hasn't overcome his fear of people, he must learn that biting or kicking (an ingrained safety mechanism for him) are unacceptable *under any circumstances*. Showing or telling him now that this is unacceptable will prevent problems later.

Halter Breaking

Halter breaking is the first step, because without control or a means of restraint, you have no influence over where the baby goes. If the foal is very young, let him stay close to his mother as you halter him the first time. Let him become accustomed to the feel of a halter on his head. Then attach a lead rope to his halter. Never let a foal learn that he can pull away from you and get free, which might happen if you try to lead him by only a halter.

Ask a friend to lead the mare as you follow with the baby. Initially, the foal will follow the mare as you "lead" him. However, don't let him pull away from you or run past you. Try to make this an easy lesson, but teach him right from wrong, even at this early age. Have your friend stop the mare and stop the baby by her side. Each and every time you stop, say the word "Whoa!" Use light tugs and releases on your lead rope to enforce to the foal that "Whoa!" means to stop and stand. Be sure to release all pressure on the rope as soon as the foal stops. This tells him that he responded correctly. The release of pressure is his reward for stopping. Never say the word for anything but a complete stop and stand. "Whoa!" is your safety word throughout a horse's life. He'll learn the meaning of the word now, and if you don't abuse it, it will stay with him throughout his life.

Always work your foal in a rock–free area, especially if he is small and not quite steady on his feet. On the slight chance that a foal will pull back (or rear) and go over backward, hold the lead rope up to keep his head up off the ground. Hitting his head on a rock as he falls could cause serious injury or death. Choose your training area with care.

Weanling

If your weanling has not been handled, you may need the help of another experienced horse person to put a halter on him the first time or two. Put the colt in a stall or a small pen and get him against a wall. Have one person grasp the foal around the chest with one hand and lift his tail over his back with the other. This will immobilize the foal, giving the second person time to slip a properly sized halter on the foal's head.

Once you have a halter on the foal, you have the means to bring his head toward you, rather than allowing him to turn his rump toward you, where he may try to kick.

You cannot force a foal to lead or respect a lead line—you must teach him to do so. Don't get into a pulling fight with an untrained colt, because brute strength won't work. Let the colt back into a wall so that the wall behind him stops him. This is why it is best to begin your work in a large stall or small pen. Use the walls or fence to your advantage and set yourself up for success.

A foal that is panicking and fighting a lead line may rear or twist and flip over backward. Pulling on the lead line, if the foal pulls in the wrong way, can cause serious damage. If possible, let the foal move backward until he bumps the wall, which will stop him. Then give him time to settle and recover his composure.

Training takes time and patience. Allow yourself enough time so that you do not feel rushed to complete the job. Give yourself two days, two weeks, or even two months to accomplish your goal if necessary. The foal must advance at his pace, not yours.

Leading with a Rump Rope

To teach a foal to move forward on your command when leading (after following the mare for a few days if he is very young), make a rump rope out of a long, thick cotton lead rope (or you may keep a special thick cotton rope just for this purpose). Make a loop that goes around the foal's rump and under his tail as illustrated in the photographs. After deciding how big

Make a loop with the rope, tie a knot over his back, and run the end through his halter.

the loop must be to fit that particular foal, snap or tie the rope so that the loop will not tighten or slip. Once the loop is around the foal, run the free end through the foal's halter under the noseband. To teach the foal to lead, first ask him to move forward in response to a cluck. Immediately give him a light tug and release on the lead line. If the foal doesn't move forward, because he probably won't do so initially, tell him that he must move by giving a sharp tug on the rump rope.

Be sure to run the free end of your rope through his halter.

Be sure to stand to the side of a foal as you ask him to move forward, and especially when giving the sharp tug on the rump rope. Many foals will jump forward when they feel the pressure from the rump rope. Be sure that you are out of his way and ready to move forward with him, allowing him enough of the lead rope to do so. If you jerk the foal back as soon as he moves forward, you will confuse him by snapping him back. In essence, you are punishing him, when he in fact is responding correctly by moving forward.

If you stand facing a baby, then ask him to move forward, you are blocking his forward movement with your body. He'll feel as if he is being asked to walk toward what he may perceive as a threatening object—you. Teach the baby to lead—to follow alongside of you—just as an older horse would do. You wouldn't walk backward with an older horse. Teach your baby the correct way right from the start.

If you drag a colt around the pen with the rump rope, you will be teaching him to respond to the rump rope, not to the halter. Use short tugs on the rump rope after first asking with the lead rope, and only add more pressure to the rump rope if he doesn't respond. The foal should feel the sharp tug of the rump rope and come forward, rewarding himself by the release of pressure. The foal soon learns that he can avoid the tug on the rump rope by obeying the pull on the lead rope and that he can avoid the pull on the lead rope by obeying the cluck. For this reason, always use these cues in the same order. First ask with a cluck, followed by a light tug on the lead rope to tell, followed by your demand that he move forward by the rump rope.

Give the foal time to absorb your request and time to perform it. Watch a riding lesson in progress. The instructor gives the command to walk. The rider must first absorb the command to walk, then prepares to tell the horse to walk. Only then can he or she actually tell the horse to walk. Now the horse must have time to absorb the request, then prepare to walk, before finally he does walk.

Walk to the side of the foal, keeping the lead rope in one hand and the rump rope in the other, so that you may ask first, and then tell.

Give Him Time

Give your foal time to hear, to prepare, and then to obey the request before you correct him. On the same note, be sure to correct him if he doesn't respond within a reasonable time frame—about three seconds. It is important to develop this feel of timing, and it is something that you should continue to work on throughout your equine's lifetime—and yours!

As your foal progresses, try to rely on the rump rope less and less and then on the pull from the lead rope less and less. However, keep your rump rope on for a bit longer than you think you need it so that you'll have a way to correct your foal if he tries to balk or stands stubbornly in one spot. For the first few days that you ask him to lead without the rump rope, keep it handy, such as hung over your shoulder.

Also, once you feel that you can discard the rump rope totally, try to lead the foal with a lead rope that is long enough to reach around the foal's rump—one that will still allow you enough room to lead him comfortably. In this way, if you find yourself in a situation where the foal will not willingly move forward past a new scary object or obstacle, you have a way to correct him by putting the end of the lead rope around his rump. Without it, you have no way to enforce your go-forward command.

If you find yourself in the situation where a foal will not move forward and you do not have a long rope, pull him sideways, first to the left and then to the right, rather than trying to pull the foal straight forward. This will many times "unlock" a foal or horse and may make him forget why he was being stubborn. Pulling a foal or a horse straight forward seldom works because it gives a horse something to set against. Pulling side to side off-balances him, forcing him to move to recover his balance.

Tying

Once a foal respects the lead rope when he is being led, he should learn to tie easily (this is explained in more detail in Chapter 4). To begin, start with a solid wall with a tie ring attached at the height of foal's head. Initially, run the rope through the ring and hold the opposite end. In this way, you control the amount of tension on the lead line. However, don't let him learn now that he can pull back and become "untied." If he pulls more strongly than what you can hold, begin this lesson at a pole or bar where you can wrap the rope around it once, giving you more leverage and making it easier for you to hold him. If he begins to pull back, use a buggy whip and tap

Use a whip to tap your foal forward if he pulls back on the tie rope. Stop tapping as soon as he moves forward.

his hindquarters until he moves forward. Stop tapping as soon as he begins to move forward. It shouldn't take long for him to realize that if he moves forward, all pressure and punishment stop and he is much more comfortable.

Start by asking him to remain "tied" for two to three minutes, then increase the time to five or ten minutes. When you see that he respects the rope and doesn't pull back, you may begin to tie him, always using a quick-release knot. Never tie a rope so long that he can get a foot over it or become tangled in it. Don't leave him unattended—keep a watchful eye on him and be prepared to use your whip to tap him forward if he begins to pull back. Be sure that you are not in a position where he can reach you if he kicks. If he does kick at you for any reason, punish him immediately by using the whip on his hindquarters in addition to using a gruff "Quit!" Teach him now that kicking is *not* acceptable.

Grooming

The next step, one that you may have already been incorporating into his daily lessons, is to teach your foal to accept being groomed and touched all over. Don't omit this step, because it prepares a colt for a saddle and pad when he becomes of an age to ride. Rub up and down his barrel, paying particular attention to where the girth will lie. Be sure to prepare the colt for a bridle by touching his ears, cheeks, and nose.

Picking Up His Feet

Next he must learn to pick up his feet. Start by having a helper hold his head. Later, after his initial lessons and once he ties well, you may tie him as you groom him and pick up his feet. Begin by running your hand up and down the foal's legs—front and back, as well as left and right. Many foals accept this easily; however, some do not. Be extremely careful of your face, especially around the hind legs.

When you work on his front legs, stand by his neck as you bend over to run your hand up and down his leg. When you work on the back legs, stay by his shoulder, because this will keep you out of kicking range. Be alert to his reaction and do not make any sudden movements that may frighten him.

After the foal accepts having his legs touched, begin to ask him to pick them up briefly. Start by picking up each front leg three times and then proceeding to his back legs. Run your hand down his leg and squeeze lightly at the back of his pastern. Be prepared to lift the foot as soon as you feel the shift in his weight as he lifts that leg the first time or two. If he

Stand by the colt's shoulder to lift a hind leg. Watch out for your face!

stands stubbornly with all four feet braced on the ground, you may gently lean into his shoulder to push his weight to the other side. This should free that leg enough so that you can now pick it up.

Once you've picked up a leg, never put it down when the foal is fighting you. Hold it and wait for that brief second when he gives in (you'll feel his leg relax in your hand). Only then should you release his leg and let him put it down. This tells the foal that he cannot "take" his leg away from you—he must wait for you to release it. He only needs to give in for a brief second before you reward him by letting him put his foot down. Don't try to force him to hold it up for too long of a period of time or he may become resentful (or unbalanced and then will have to put his foot down).

Don't think that because he picks up a front leg, he'll automatically pick up a hind leg, or that because he picks up his legs on the left side, he'll also pick up his legs on the right side. He must be taught to pick up all four legs on command—front and back, both left and right.

When you progress to a hind leg and find that the colt tries to kick at you, find a long (eight- to ten-foot) thick, soft cotton lead rope (or any soft rope). Carefully loop it around behind the foal's hind pastern. If you cannot safely reach down and place the rope around his pastern, take one end of the rope and run it between his hind legs, as high up as you can, keeping hold of either end. Don't tie the rope—just hold each side so that you can drop it if you must. The rope will now be on either side of his leg and you may carefully let it slide down into position. After the rope is around his pastern, say the words "pick it up," then pull his leg forward, lifting it toward you with the rope. Stay safely by his shoulder, out of kicking range, and let the rope do the work. Hold the leg in the air with the rope briefly, then let it down. Scratch the foal's rump to reward him for that brief instant of holding his foot in the air. However, if he kicks at or fights the rope, continue to hold it and let him fight it out. As soon as he gives in and relaxes, let his foot down. Initially, don't physically touch the leg with your hand.

When he comfortably picks up his foot as you pull it forward with the rope (and this may take one day or two weeks), then—and only then—grasp his hind foot with your hand after you have picked it up by pulling it to you with the rope. Again, praise him with a kind word and scratch his rump for obeying. Once he accepts this step readily, then pick up his foot with your hand, keeping your face out of kicking range. Pick up each foot three times, then move to the next one. After picking up all four feet three times, end your lesson or go on to another one. Remember that if the foal fights, you must hold that leg briefly until he gives in. If he pulls the leg out of your hand, pick it up once or twice again, or until he gives in. Let him know that putting the foot down was *your* idea, not his.

CHAPTER THREE

Choosing a Discipline for Your Colt

———————— ◆ ————————

I f you buy a colt to train, first look at his conformation, train-ability, and way of going with the goal that you have in mind for him. If your goal is to work toward owning the next world-champion reining horse or dressage horse, then that colt must first have the ability to reach that same goal. If you breed your best mare to a stallion of a different type of discipline than what you have in mind and you believe that you can train the newborn foal to excel at a certain event, you may be wasting both time and effort. You can invest all of the time, money, and talent you wish into a colt, and yet, if the colt is not capable (because of mental or physical limitations), he will not be able to excel at that discipline. He may excel at another, but if it doesn't match your goal, you will be trying to force a colt into something for which he is not naturally suited.

After you train a colt for thirty to sixty days, ask yourself the following questions:

- Is he trainable? Does he have a good "mind" and is he will-ing to learn?
- What would his conformation make him best suited for?

- What is his athletic ability?
- How does he move?

Let's examine each of these questions more thoroughly.

IS HE TRAINABLE?

A colt with perfect conformation that will not accept training procedures will never utilize his true potential. If a colt fights you every chance that he gets or does not retain what he was previously taught, he will never become well trained. Some horses may fight you momentarily (or for a number of days or weeks), then give in, perform as required, and retain what they were taught. These horses may go on to prove themselves, although you will have to work harder at training them.

A few horses seem to learn so easily that you wonder if you even have to train them. This trait (a good mind) should be a goal of breeders, because it makes the entire training process less stressful to both the colt and his trainer. A pretty colt that cannot or will not learn will not compare to a less attractive colt that learns easily.

If you choose to train a colt for a more demanding discipline, it is important that he have a good mind and a high level of trainability. While a Western pleasure colt must have the

When choosing a reining prospect, be sure that he has the mind, athletic ability, and conformation to be a reiner. This is Cals Pistol, past winner of the Senior Reining at the Congress and the sire of Caloola.

ability to remain unruffled under pressure, the demands or stress that are placed on him are not as high as those that are placed on a reining colt. An English horse used for flat classes will not need to have the same level of mind and ability as a jumper or a top-level dressage horse.

For a colt to be trainable, he must not only accept the training process without fighting it excessively, he must also remember what he was previously taught. If you spent an entire lesson teaching your colt to walk calmly over a bridge, yet he comes out the next day and acts as if he's never seen the bridge before, how long will it take you to train this colt? Can this colt be trained? If you teach your colt one thing on one day, does he remember it the next time or must you retrain him every time you mount?

Trainability in a colt will begin to show prior to your riding him. You will see signs as you begin to longe or ground drive a colt. Some may fool you, but you'll get a good idea of how your initial training will progress. Stay alert. Notice the reactions of a colt as you work him. The more colts that you work, the more you'll notice how each reacts differently to the same training procedure.

On occasion—and you'll see this more with the demanding disciplines—you may find that a colt accepts the beginning levels of training with ease, only to hit a slump or block that he cannot get past. Many colts continue to learn for days, then hit a week or a month where they seem to stay at the same level. This may be related to age and he may only need more time to mature mentally. Others, however are unable to get past a certain stage of training. With this type of colt, train him as far as you can, see what he is best suited for, and find him a home doing that if he is unsuitable for your chosen discipline.

WHAT IS HIS CONFORMATION?

You ask this question so that you can determine what the colt is best suited for. My initial reaction to a long-strided, tall Thoroughbred is that he should excel at the English flat classes or the hunter or jumper classes. A short-strided Quarter Horse with flat (or no) knee action would fit the bill for a Western

Eternal Impression, Paint Stallion owned by Terry Morgan, McMinnville, Tennessee. This stallion has twenty-eight halter points and eleven grands.

pleasure horse. A good-looking, stocky, heavily muscled Quarter Horse should do well at halter classes and an Arab with good bone may be the perfect endurance horse. A fine-boned Arab that doesn't have an excessive amount of flashy action may be suited for the Arab country pleasure classes and a good-strided Morgan may make an excellent driving horse.

While there are exceptions to every rule—and I'm generalizing for the sake of showing that every horse usually fits at least one discipline—looking at basic conformation will give you an idea of the colt's capabilities. His conformation not only tells you if he is suited to the type of work that you are asking of him, it will also tell you if he is able to hold up to the demands placed on him by that discipline. A colt that is not physically suited to a certain discipline will not only become sore, his mind will become resentful because his body will hurt when he is asked to perform certain maneuvers. He will not tolerate this kind of "abuse" for long without reacting.

LOOK AT HIS ATHLETIC ABILITY

Athletic ability is the colt's ability to move easily and agilely. A colt that is "light" on his feet will more readily be able to perform the more demanding maneuvers, such as reining, dressage, hunting, or jumping. A colt that hits the ground too

Vozza, TB, owned by L. Lambrose, Norfolk, Connecticut. A hunter should have the mind, stride or movement, and ability to be a hunter.

hard, usually because of his conformation, is uncomfortable to ride and he will not have the natural ability to perform certain maneuvers. It will be difficult for him to perform the more demanding events and it will place extra stress on his bones and muscles. A colt needs to have the natural ability to perform the demands placed on him by the chosen disciplines. Training can only overcome so much.

HOW DOES HE MOVE?

A long-strided, flat–kneed colt looks the part of a hunter under saddle. He seems to glide over the ground, making it look effortless. The same type of colt may be naturally suited to jump fences. However, a hunter or jumper also needs to have power in his hind legs to propel himself over four-foot-high fences as he folds up his front legs. While many horses can be taught to jump, some are naturally more athletic than others. A colt that prefers to keep all four feet on the ground is not suited for life as a jumper. On the same note, a colt that is basically lazy will probably become resentful when he is forced into putting all that effort into lifting himself up and over fences. He'll more than likely knock down quite a few of them as he learns that it hurts less to clear them than to knock them down.

A prospective reining colt that cannot get his own feet out of the way will not be able to perform the high-speed turn-arounds or spins required in today's competitive showing world. A reiner that cannot reach under himself with his hind legs will not be able to elevate his shoulders enough to slide to a spectacular show-stopping stop, nor will he be able to change leads correctly and effortlessly.

A fine carriage horse that drags his toes along the ground does not have the dazzle required to win today. A carriage horse must show a lot of flashy action. Some of this can be helped by shoeing techniques, but it is the horse that must have the inherent will and ability to put on a "show."

EVALUATE YOUR COLT

Keeping all of this information in mind as you ride your colt will allow you to make a proper choice for his discipline. The decision doesn't have to be made in the first thirty days; you may find that after six months or even a year your colt is better suited for one thing activity than another. Always be open to change. Let your colt tell you what he is best suited for. You may find that halfway through your training program,

Sunny, gray gelding owned by Joyce Smilie, Watertown, Connecticut, and ridden by Bob Porzio. A roping horse should have good bone to hold up to the demands placed on him and must have cow sense.
Photo by Laurie Truskauskas

your colt shines at an event that is not what you initially had in mind. He may like to perform one discipline rather than another. Some horses are versatile and can perform several different types of events confidently.

Sometimes it is just trial and error to see which discipline suits your particular colt. Again, some horses change as they mature. Sometimes a colt's mind cannot handle the demands placed on him at a young age, but if you take it slow and try a year later, you may find that he picks it up with no problem.

Not all horses are suited to be show horses, just as many horse owners will never want to see the inside of a show ring. Some horses are happiest on the trail, either because of being soured on too much ring work or just not being able to handle the demands or stress placed on them by constant ring work or training. They are content hacking along the trails, enjoying nature. A quiet horse that is not easily ruffled is a joy to work around and can teach a newly addicted horse person to ride. The rider is happy, and the colt is happy, and that is what horses are all about. These quiet, dependable horses also make good lead horses. They teach the more skittish youngsters that bridges are safe, that monsters do not leap out of running streams, that drain culverts on the edges of roads do not hide horse-eating trolls, and that cars are not things to run from.

Light horses (as well as the draft breeds) can be used for pulling plows, wagons, and carts, or for logging. A team of horses will not tear up the ground like a large dozer. In addition, the draft-horse breeds are now gaining in popularity as riding horses because of their quiet, easygoing attitude. Not much spooks a draft horse out on a trail, making the ride a pleasant, safe, and stress–free experience.

Horses are also being used in handicapped riding programs, teaching children to walk again because of the similarity of motion. They also teach these children the importance of grooming, not only for the horses, but for themselves as well.

Looking at a few of the horses that I've trained recently, one screams, "I'm a hunter!" He's a long-strided, good-moving,

San Leo Scarlet, Quarter Horse gelding owned by Laurie Truskauskas, Athens, Texas. This horse is quite versatile and makes a nice all-around Western horse. Photo by Laurie Truskauskas

16.2–hand Appendix Quarter Horse. Another murmurs, "Western pleasure." She's a somewhat short-strided, flat-kneed, good-moving half Arab, half Quarter Horse. Another, a seven-year–old Arab, snorts, "Endurance! You can't tire me out!" He has a relentless inner drive coupled with good bone suited to hold up to the demands placed on such a horse by the fifty- to one-hundred-mile rides. Another chants, "Reiner." He's extremely athletic, very responsive, and exceptionally willing to please. He has a long hip to enable him to get down into the ground and slide, he's straight-legged, so he will not "spread-eagle" when he slides, and he has strong hocks that should keep him sound throughout a demanding career. And another drawls, "I'm a trail horse. Let's take our time, look at nature, and go for a leisurely stroll through the woods. Don't get excited—that's only water, or only a bridge, or any number of obstacles that might spook a lesser horse."

There is nothing physically wrong with any of these horses. They're young, under five, and have an entire life in front of them. But if you listen and pay attention, each horse will either shout or whisper what he is best suited for. There is nothing wrong with your colt if he will not, or physically cannot, perform your chosen discipline. Rather than trying to force him into being something that he's not, either change your discipline or buy a colt that is better suited for the discipline that you choose. Asking a colt to do work that he is not readily suited for is like trying to ask a sweet, slim, petite twelve-year-old girl to work construction, shoveling blacktop eight hours a day. How long do you think she'll want to, or be able to, perform this work? Would you ask an energetic young boy to sit quietly at a desk for twelve hours? While some people (just like horses) are forced into the wrong profession, the odds are against them being happy doing it.

LOOK AT YOUR COLT

Take a good look at a colt's conformation, willingness to learn, and suitability to each discipline before you try to force him into something that he cannot be. If you do not have the knowledge or the background to select the best candidate for the job you have in mind, or the knowledge to decipher your colt's inclinations, ask for professional help. The money spent now can save you time, money, and effort down the road. Working with your colt, not against him, will make the entire training procedure less stressful to both of you.

Tying a Horse Safely with a Quick-Release Knot

◆

Teaching a foal or horse to tie correctly should be taught to every young horse and then be reinforced throughout a horse's life. Every foal or horse should be taught to tie and should stand quietly when tied. A horse or foal must learn to respect the tie rope without pulling back, fussing or fidgeting. In addition to enjoying the benefits of tying a horse so that you may tack him up safely (without him moving from side to side or trying to move away from the saddle) teaching a horse to stand tied teaches him patience. A horse learns that it is in his best interest to stand quietly. A ring, post, or tree is not as forgiving as a human might be, and the horse will not gain relief from fighting the tie rope when he is tied to a solid object (as he might if a person were holding him).

Teaching a horse to stand quietly when tied will help him later when you ask him to stand quietly when he is mounted. A horse that fidgets when tied will most likely fidget when he is mounted and asked to stand for long periods of time. The length of time a horse remains tied should be increased gradually. I tie my babies for five to ten minutes and increase the time to an hour or so once a colt comes of age to saddle break. Leaving a horse tied while he is still tacked can teach him that work

45

does not always end when his lesson is over. This is helpful for the horse that is headed for the show circuit or for the horse that has misbehaved and/or that needs to be ridden a second time on that day. A horse that rushes back to the barn will find that the barn is not a pleasant place to be if he is left standing tacked up for an hour or more after returning home.

TYING TEACHES RESPECT

A horse that has been taught to tie will have more respect for a lead line unless he is taught differently by a handler. People actually "teach" horses that it is acceptable for the horse to pull people around by not enforcing respect for the lead line. A horse learns that a solid object has no give to it, and most will not continue to test it, yet a horse soon differentiates between standing tied and being led by a person, especially a person that doesn't demand respect. Teach a horse to tie and then keep him respectful of the lead line by enforcing correct behavior at all times.

Teaching a foal to stand tied is beneficial because he doesn't yet have the strength that an older horse has to fight the tie rope. But never underestimate the power of a 200- or 300-pound foal. Use a strong rope, work under safe conditions and be sure to watch closely so that he doesn't pull back and injure

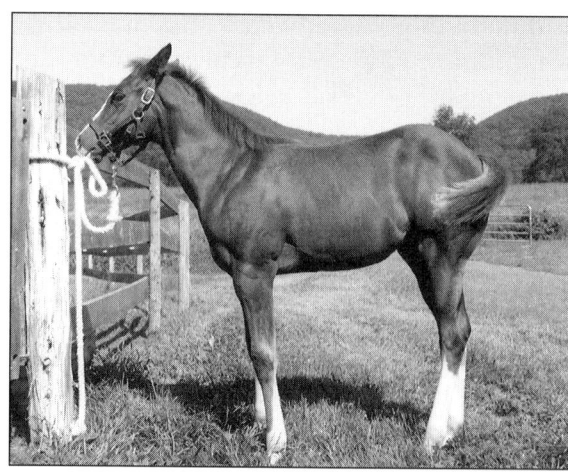

All horses, young and old, must learn to tie.

his neck. Most young foals give in sooner, because they haven't had two or three years of freedom to overcome. They accept the restriction to their head somewhat easier. Teaching a colt to stand quietly now (when tied) will help later when you begin to use this horse—when he needs to stand tied in cross-ties to get tacked up, to stand quietly next to the trailer at a horse show, or to stand on a picket line on an overnight trail ride.

QUICK-RELEASE KNOT

Always tie with a quick-release knot—in the case of an emergency. You may use the method shown here or purchase one of the tie straps with panic snaps on the end like those that are used in cross ties or trailer ties. I recommend the quick-release knot when teaching a horse to tie, because the metal panic snaps can snap back into your face. I know of one incident with that type of snap where a girl's finger was broken while she was trying to release a panicking horse. *Your safety should always come first.*

The method explained here will work with almost any type of rope lead line, provided it is long enough to tie this knot and still allow your horse to have eighteen inches of rope from his halter to the tie. (I like my lead ropes to be at least eight feet in length.)

LENGTH OF TIE ROPE

Never tie a horse with longer than eighteen inches of rope from the halter to the tie. A horse can get a foot over a rope or his head under the rope. Most horses will panic when they feel a pull from the rope from an unexpected source, such as over their neck, rather than from the halter ring. A horse that is tied too short will be too restricted and may panic.

I tie my horses at wither height. Tying lower than this allows a horse to get a foot over a rope and pulls his head down at an awkward angle if he begins to fight the rope.

When I first teach a young foal to tie, I take one or two wraps around a post and hold the other end of the rope. I can then evaluate the foal's reaction to being tied. Usually, if a foal has been taught to lead, being tied for a few minutes is no big deal. On the chance that a foal puts up a big fight, having a helper hold the end of the line while standing in a safe spot allows you to get behind the foal and tap him forward with a longe whip. As soon as the foal steps forward, be sure to stop tapping. He'll soon find that the pressure on his head is released and the tapping stops when he steps forward and gives in. If he pulls back, repeat the procedure. Start with about five minutes per session and work up to ten. Once a foal accepts this, you may tie him with a quick-release knot, still watching him and being prepared to send him forward.

This same method will work with a two-year-old or an older horse, with the exception of holding the end of the rope. With a horse that is too strong to hold, make two wraps around the post to which he is tied. Fifteen to twenty feet away, make your quick-release knot around a second post or tree. Using this method will allow the horse to think that he is tied to the post directly in front of him. Tying to a post fifteen to twenty feet away will keep you or your helper out of harm's way, if it becomes necessary to untie the horse. Keep your longe whip handy and use as much force as necessary, starting with the least amount and increasing it as the need dictates, to send the horse forward. He must learn that the pressure on the lead line stops when he moves forward. When using a whip on a horse, hit him below the tail on the buttocks. Hitting lower than this can cause a horse to kick and may allow your whip to become tangled around his legs.

USE THE CORRECT EQUIPMENT

Always tie a horse to a solid post, tree, or tie ring. Use a strong post that will not break and cannot be moved by a struggling equine. Be sure that the area surrounding your tied horse is free of obstacles that could hurt him or that could be knocked over and cause him to spook.

Never tie a horse to a gate. I once saw a horse tearing across a pasture with his head tied securely to a twelve-foot-long metal gate. The horse could only be caught after the gate got stuck between a tree and a rock and the rope broke. The horse had some serious cuts and scrapes that had to be stitched. If this horse had been tied to a solid object, as he should have been, this entire disaster could have been prevented. Use well-made equipment attached to a solid post or to a place made specifically to hold a 1,000-pound equine. This prevents the horse from breaking a halter or lead rope and learning that he can free himself by pulling back. It is easier to teach a horse to respect being tied and to tie correctly from the beginning than it is to try to retrain a confirmed puller.

Never tie a horse with a chain over (or under) his nose. If the horse pulls back while tied in that manner, the chain will "bite" into the underside of his nose. A horse will then pull back harder to get away from the pain. The links of a chain can put permanent bumps on a horse's nose, damaging the soft cartilage located there, or cut and damage the soft skin under his nose.

Never tie a horse to anything with bridle reins, even if you use a quick-release knot. This could cause serious harm to the bars of a horse's mouth or to his teeth. A well-made halter and lead line will, in most cases, hold a 1,000–pound horse; a bridle will not.

I use a quick-release knot religiously. Whether a horse is young or old, big or small, I use this knot. When you initially teach any horse to tie, use a strong lead rope with a strong snap attached to a heavy-duty nylon or leather halter. Tie the rope to a strong, safe post.

TYING A QUICK-RELEASE KNOT

Whether you are tying your horse to a solid object so that he will stay in one place, or you are tying one rein to his girth to teach him to give his head to bit pressure, use a quick-release knot in case the horse gets into trouble. If he does start to pull back, rearing and stepping over a rope, or fighting so much that you fear for his safety, you'll have a quick and easy way to release him. Get into the habit now of always tying a horse with a quick-release knot—you'll never know when you may need it. To keep the knot from becoming too tight if a horse decides to test it, take two wraps around the post before tying the knot. This way, the stress is on the rope, not on the knot. A word of caution: Although this knot is easy to undo in most circumstances, if a 1,000–pound horse really sets back and puts all of his weight onto the rope for an extended period of time, he can tighten the knot so much that it sometimes takes a strong person to undo it. For this reason, it is best to always keep a sharp knife handy in an easily accessible place, just in case. For the most part, however, this knot will provide you with a way to untie an unruly horse safely.

To tie a quick-release knot:

1. Put your rope around the post to which the horse is to be tied. In photo 1, the right section of the rope is tied to the horse, and the left section is the free end.
2. Make a loop with the free end by bringing the farthest section of the rope under the end closest to the pole as shown.
3. Put the loop that you just made under the section of rope that is to be tied to the horse.
4. Now put your right hand in position to grasp the free end of the rope to prepare to bring it through the first loop.
5. Then pull that section of the rope through your original loop.
6. . . .which makes another loop.
7. Pull the knot tight by placing your left hand over it (which is really the first loop) and pulling the second loop until the first loop tightens. To tighten the knot so that it stays at the correct height on the pole and doesn't slide to the bottom, pull the end tied to the horse as you place your hand close to the knot. This will slide the entire knot close to the pole, much like a slip knot slides.
8. To release the knot, all you have to do is pull the free end (the end on the left in the photo), which causes the knot to slide back through the first loop until the knot is untied and the horse is free.

Tying the quick-release knot.

You may find it easier to reverse the process. Rather than have the right section of the rope (as shown here) tied to the horse, reverse the order and tie the left side to the horse. Then make your first loop with the right section of the rope and continue with the directions, substituting left for right. Be sure to always bring the rope *under,* as stated, or your quick-release knot will not come out as it should.

Longeing the Young Colt

◆

The first step that actually prepares a colt to be ridden is longeing. Training a colt to longe before you ride allows you to teach him specific cues to walk, trot/jog, and canter or lope. Teaching these cues from the ground will make it easier for the colt to understand when you mount the first time that he should jog when you cluck and lope when you kiss. Colts that respect "Whoa!" on the longe line will almost always stop from the same command when they are mounted the first time.

Never pull on the reins of any horse to stop. Lightly lift the reins to signal a stop, rather than force the horse to stop. A colt must learn the rein signal before a rein cue will be effective in stopping him. Using a verbal command as he learns the rein aids will keep his mouth soft and responsive for later use, and will make it easier for the colt to understand your request. Never abuse the whoa command on the ground by saying "Whoa!" unless you *mean* "Whoa!" Only saying "Whoa!" for a complete halt will teach the colt that he must come to a complete halt whenever he hears the word. For safety reasons, this is the most important command that you can teach any horse. When you begin to ride this colt, the same command may be the difference between an uneventful ride and a disaster.

BEGINNING TO LONGE

Longeing a colt means that the colt will go around you in a circle on command. This is something that you must teach a colt because it is not a natural procedure for him. Take your time and show the colt what you want, and he will soon understand.

Before asking any colt to move off in a longeing circle, first spend a few minutes rubbing the longe whip over his entire body. The colt must understand that the whip is an aid. It is not something to be punished with or something to fear. Spend as much time as necessary rubbing the whip over the colt's body until he accepts it as a training aid. Rub the whip along his sides, over his rump, up and down his neck and along his legs. Never put yourself in a position that is unsafe where the colt could lash out and kick you or strike at you with a front leg. Stay on the *side* of the colt and keep control of his head. Talk quietly while you rub the whip gently on his neck, hindquarters, and legs. Once he accepts this new training aid, progress to longeing.

To teach the colt to longe, stand with your body in line with his hip. This is extremely important. Standing in the wrong position is the reason for most failed longing attempts. Standing in front of the horse blocks his forward movement. Body position or body language is important and something that horses understand more easily than we do.

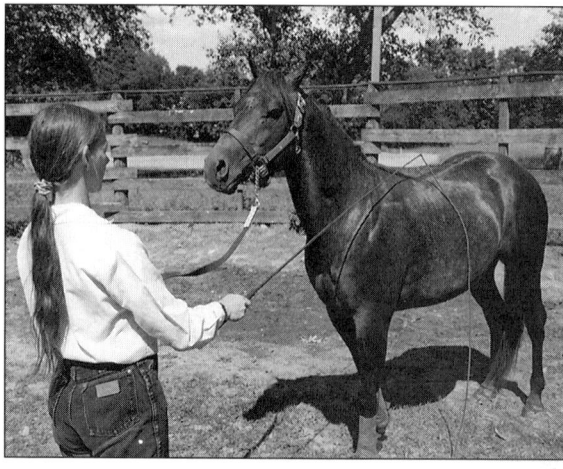

Before longeing, spend a few minutes rubbing the colt with the whip.

Because I've gotten in front of the colt, he tries to turn in and face me. Correct this by walking back to his hip.

Make a "V" with the longe line in your left hand and the whip in your right hand.

To longe to the left, hold the longe line in your left hand with the whip in your right hand. If you drew an imaginary line from your right hand to his rump and your left hand to his head, it would make a "V". Reverse the longe line and whip to go in the opposite direction. Start off with the longe line fairly short, but not so short that you are close to the colt's hindquarters where he may be able to kick you. Coil the balance of the longe line in your hand. Don't let it drag on the ground or you might trip on it, creating a dangerous situation. Also, never wrap the line tightly around your hand. If a horse or colt spooks, you'll get dragged.

Tell your colt to "walk" as you gently swish the whip on the ground or tap his hindquarters with the whip to tell him to move forward. The first day that you longe your colt, you may need to continually walk toward his hip as your longe line guides his front in what may be a somewhat lopsided circle. After a day or so, he should begin to understand and go around you in a more correct circle. Take your time and show the colt what you want. This early training sets the tone for the balance of a horse's life under saddle. Be patient.

TEACHING THE CUES

As soon as the colt starts to walk, immediately stop tapping and let him walk around you in the longeing circle. Let the line out slowly, loop by loop, to increase the size of your circle as the colt understands to circle around you. After a week or two of longeing, give the colt enough line so that he is about five feet away from the rail if you are working in a round pen. Keeping him off the fence makes him pay attention to you and teaches him not to depend on the rail.

As the colt understands to go forward around you when he is asked to longe, begin to teach the cues for the various gaits, such as a cluck for a jog or trot and a kiss for a canter or lope. By using these cues consistently, you will later be able to free longe the colt, and it will also help when you mount for the first time. To ask the colt to jog, cluck first. If he doesn't respond, snap the whip behind him to tell him to jog. Fit your cues to the colt. If he's very responsive, a swish on the ground may be enough to make him jog. If he's a quiet colt, a loud snap from the whip behind him may be necessary. Enforce the cue if necessary so that the colt learns from the beginning that he must respect you and your cues *and go forward on command.* This will benefit both you and the colt when you begin to ride him.

Once the colt is jogging, stand quietly and turn in a small circle so that the colt is always in front of you. Keep your eyes and concentration on him. Don't talk to people outside the pen or you'll confuse him. Horses know when your attention is not on them. The colt must learn to obey your commands, so start him correctly from the beginning.

Let the colt go around the pen a couple of times until he's relaxed and moving freely. Only after he's made two to four circles should you ask for a transition to another gait. If you ask him to change gaits too soon, he may think that he is being corrected for doing something wrong. Giving him time to settle and relax at each gait will let him mentally absorb the cue. He'll soon realize that you leave him alone when he responds correctly—the basis for all training. Only snap the whip when the colt needs to be told to continue at his current speed or to increase his speed. Snapping the whip when the colt is performing correctly will only confuse him. *Your every action should tell him something. Your inaction means that he is performing as desired.*

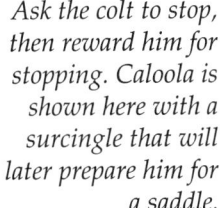

Ask the colt to stop, then reward him for stopping. Caloola is shown here with a surcingle that will later prepare him for a saddle.

To ask for a lope, make a kissing noise. Add the whip cue if he doesn't respond. Again, ask first, then "tell" him, then enforce your command if necessary. If the colt lopes at least four or five strides and then breaks back to a jog, say "Jog" and cluck—the cue to jog. Do this as soon as he starts to jog. With much repetition, he'll associate the word "jog" with slowing to a jog from a lope. Once he's moving in a relaxed manner at the jog, kiss to ask him to lope again. Make him lope for a couple of circles, then allow him to break to a jog or a walk. If he jogs, repeat the above-mentioned sequence of cues. If he walks, say "Walk" and let him walk around you in the longeing circle.

GOING TOO FAST

If the colt is speeding around you at a gallop, use your voice in a soothing tone to say "Easy, easy, easy." If he doesn't respond to that, ease him into a smaller circle with the longe line. A smaller circle forces him to go slower to keep his balance. When he reaches the desired level of speed, stop saying "easy" and let the colt continue at the desired speed, leaving him alone when he is correct.

It will take time for the colt to absorb these new cues. You must be consistent so that the colt will associate clucking with jogging and kissing with loping (or trotting or cantering). In the beginning, don't be overly concerned if the colt slows down on his own if he is so inclined. Time your verbal commands with his breaking to a slower gait (or increasing to a faster gait). After two or three weeks, the colt should begin to respond more readily to your cues to increase or decrease his speed. However, do be sure that he will increase his speed from time to time when you ask him to do so.

TEACHING "WHOA!"

To teach the colt to stop, wait until near the end of your lesson. Let him work off his excess energy before asking him to stop and stand. Let him settle to a walk or jog. Then, at a point away from the gate, say "Whoa!" Give the colt a moment to respond. If he continues to move, snap (or give a sharp tug and release) on the longe line. Repeat the whoa command *once* as you tug. If the colt continues to move, pull the line hard enough so that the colt faces you. Say "Whoa!" once in a meaningful voice. When the colt stops, quickly praise him verbally in a soft tone of voice. Walk up to his neck and rub him. Let him know that stopping was the correct response by rewarding him with a brief rest.

When I first ask a colt to stop, I say "Whoa!" one time without an accompanying correction from the longe line. I give him a chance to respond. If he doesn't stop, I then use a corrective snap in addition to saying "Whoa!" one more time. Never say "Whoa!" softly over and over. Say it once like you mean it, then enforce it. I will use a chain under his chin a few times to reinforce that "Whoa!" means to stop immediately. Obeying the whoa command is extremely important, and I strictly enforce it. All of my colts obey it without question.

When the colt stops, reward him with a brief rest.

If the colt pulls on the longe line while circling, give a sharp tug and then release. Continue to pull and release, pull and release, until the colt circles without pulling on the longe line. Don't try to outpull him and don't let him pull *you* around the arena. That is a form of disobedience and must be corrected. Make him respect you.

Never ask for a change of pace or stop him in front of the gate. You don't want him to think of the gate as a place to stop or as a way out. Also, never ask a colt to stop in a place where he has tried to stop before on his own. Make him wait for and respect your cues. When he halts correctly on your command at a point away from the gate, walk up to him, praise him, then lead him across the pen and out.

Longeing with a saddle prepares a colt for being ridden.

GOOD BEHAVIOR

Reward good behavior, not bad behavior. Look for slight improvement when you are ending a lesson, keeping in mind that colts have a short attention span. I usually longe a young horse for ten to twenty minutes at a time. Longeing a young colt in a small circle stresses his legs because of the smallness of the circle. Keep your lessons brief if the foal is young.

CONSISTENCY

As pointed out in Chapter 1, consistency is a key to successful training and it is definitely critical in longeing. I use a cluck for a jog and a kiss for a lope. I say "walk" when I want the colt to walk and the word "easy" when I want the colt to slow in a given gait. While you may change the words to suit yourself (such as using "trot" or "canter"), it is extremely important to use the same cues each time.

FREE LONGEING

When a colt understands these cues on the longe line and responds correctly most of the time, I begin to free longe a colt. I teach this the same way I do with the longe line. Unsnap the longe line or lead rope only after you get to the round pen. Never lead a colt (or horse) by his halter without a lead rope. If

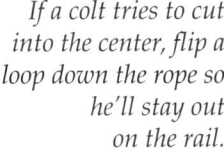

If a colt tries to cut into the center, flip a loop down the rope so he'll stay out on the rail.

he pulls back and gets away, as can easily happen without a lead line, you have just taught him the beginning of a bad habit. If he gets away with it two or three times, it is a habit and now must be broken. Set yourself up for success by not taking unnecessary chances.

When you begin to free longe a colt, he may jog or lope instead of walk. Use the appropriate cue for those gaits as if it was your idea. When he slows, again use the corresponding cue. In time, he should respond to your cues to increase or decrease his speed if you have been consistent in teaching him. If your colt doesn't stop from the whoa command when you are free longeing, immediately put him back on the longe line. Repeat the sequence of "Whoa!" cues. Ask or tell him to stop every third or fourth circle, then reward him for stopping. After a week or two, try free longeing again. If he won't stop, go right back to the longe line and make him stop. Don't give a colt the chance to pick up a bad habit.

CHANGE DIRECTIONS WHILE FREE LONGEING

To ask a colt to reverse when free longeing, stop him at a point away from the gate. Then step from your position in line with his hip to a point that is in line with his shoulder. Use your longe whip as an extension of your arm. Place the whip in front of him and cluck to send him in the other direction. Then proceed with your cues to walk, jog, and lope in the opposite direction. Work both directions equally, or spend additional time on his stiffer or less obedient side.

Most horses learn free longeing easily if you have been consistent in your cues. The horse or colt benefits from free longeing by being allowed to move in a natural position. When free longeing in the round pen, the colt's head and neck are not cocked to the inside, as with a longe line. This allows the colt to carry himself straighter with his weight more evenly balanced.

FUTURE TRAINING

I begin to prepare a colt for his future training under saddle after I've taught him to longe. I don't necessarily wait until he free longes, but I do like to teach the horse to free longe at some point. When I later begin to teach a horse to "give" to the bit, I find it easier to free longe rather than having the encumbrance of a longe line attached to a halter over a bridle.

The next step is saddling and bridling a colt for the first time. This is an important step for preparing a colt to be ridden. Carrying a saddle teaches him to carry weight and to tolerate a girth being tightened around his barrel. Most colts react more strongly to being saddled and longed for the first time than they do to actually being mounted for the first time. Usually after a few longeing sessions, a colt adjusts to flapping stirrups and the movement of the saddle on his back. Longeing is an important step in a colt's training, because it teaches him respect for your cues. By asking the colt to carry a saddle while longeing, after he knows how to longe, you are preparing him for a future rider.

CHAPTER SIX

Saddling and Bridling Your Colt the First Time

◆

L ongeing your colt while he is tacked with both saddle and bridle will help to prepare him to be ridden at a future date. Many people think that the first time you ride a colt, he will buck and put on a big show. But this seldom happens. In general, if a colt is going to buck, it will be when he finds that the saddle strapped to his back doesn't come off, usually when he is longed with the saddle the first time. He *must* learn that the saddle is on to stay. No matter how hard he bucks, leaps, or rears (if he has a mind to do so), he must learn that the saddle remains. Although I recommend using an old saddle that can take abuse, for the rare colt that might rear and flip over backwards, be sure that the latigo straps and girth are in good condition and that they will stand up to whatever tricks the colt may try.

By following the logical sequence outlined in this book, most colts accept being ridden quite readily and they become prepared both mentally and physically. Most of them walk, jog, and lope quietly the first day that they are ridden, even if they bucked a time or two when they were first saddled.

Remember that early ground training lays the foundation for future training under saddle. This includes teaching a colt

Use an old saddle when you first saddle a colt, but be sure that your latigos and girth will hold up to whatever tricks the colt may try.

respect for a lead line and a longe line, to move forward and halt on command, and to stand quietly for grooming—in other words, trust and respect for a human handler.

WATCH YOUR COLT

Watch a colt's body language when you introduce any new object. Never stand directly in front of him because he may strike with a front leg. Watch his ears—they will tell you if he is angry (flat back), if he is listening (one or both cocked toward you), or if his attention is elsewhere (pointed in the direction in which he is interested). Learn to read a horse's body language by studying each horse that you work with. The knowledge that you gain now may save you later.

Some colts, when frightened, will push or jump into you. They look to you for safety as they did to their dam. You must teach your colt that *this is not acceptable* behavior. Put a chain under his nose and shank him (give one or two hard snaps on the lead line), or hit his chest (not his face) sharply with a crop, when he crowds you. Be sure that he understands that he must respect your space and not jump into you. *Your safety should always be your primary concern.*

Teaching a colt to accept new objects (brushes, hoof picks, clippers, and spray bottles) not only teaches him to accept grooming tools, but to trust you. In this way, when the time comes to place a saddle on his back, he should accept the saddle quietly. If you also reinforce that he must respect the whoa command, you will find it easier to saddle him the first and succeeding times. *Respect starts on the ground.*

BEFORE SADDLING

Before saddling a colt, prepare him for the saddle by rubbing a saddle blanket over his entire body. Give him time to see what you are carrying. Approach his shoulder slowly and calmly with the blanket. If you are nervous, your colt will sense it, *and he'll be nervous.* Approach him naturally, yet be alert to any signs that he may act up. Safety is your foremost concern. Hold the blanket and let him smell it. Colts are naturally curious and will examine almost anything new if they are allowed to do so. Talk quietly to reassure him that all is well. Rub the blanket up and down his neck, then over his back. Spend as much time as necessary until he accepts the blanket calmly. This may take two days or two weeks. Only after he accepts the blanket should you continue.

Approach the colt's shoulder with a saddle pad or blanket.

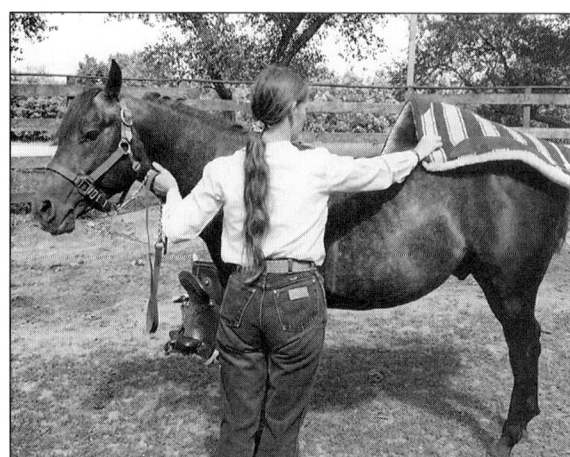

Slide the blanket over the colt's back.

If you know the bloodlines or have previously worked with colts of the same breeding, you have an advantage. Most colts of the same breeding react in a similar manner, giving you an idea of what to expect. However, if this is a new bloodline or you have never started a colt, notice how the colt reacts to each new lesson. Then plan your lessons accordingly.

EVALUATE

A colt that spooks at the littlest thing will require more time and patience on your part to lay a solid foundation. A quiet, trusting colt will usually accept a saddle easily. A spoiled colt is the hardest to train because he has very little respect for humans. Watching each colt's behavior as I approach him with new objects helps me to evaluate him, and gives me an idea of what to expect later when I begin to ride and train him.

With a spooky or nervous colt, it is easiest to start with a surcingle because it is lighter and less cumbersome than a saddle. A surcingle is also a good choice if you have never started a colt. If a saddle should slip around a colt's middle because you didn't get it tightened enough, the colt might get a foot caught in a stirrup. In any case, it will frighten the colt and set back his training. Most colts seem to react more to a girth being tightened around their barrel than to the actual weight of a saddle, and a surcingle accomplishes that same feeling of tightness.

SURCINGLE

Choose a calm day for a colt's first lesson with a surcingle. A windy, cool day will increase the likelihood of him spooking. Always set yourself up for success. Be sure that the colt is familiar with the place in which you plan to work. If you plan to take your colt to new area to start saddle breaking him, spend a few days longeing him there first. It should be a flat, enclosed area, free of objects. I prefer to start colts in a round pen. However, any flat, enclosed area will work.

I don't like to put a surcingle on a colt for the first time in a stall or barn aisle because if he blows up, I want to have room to move out of the way. Also, a select few may rear and go over backwards when they feel a girth tightened around their barrel. If they hit their head on a cement floor, or wall (or rock, if outside), they could become seriously injured. Always think ahead for possible problems.

Use a cotton longe line; nylon can burn your hands. Using a longe line will allow you to maintain control from a distance if a colt panics. A lead line keeps you too close to the colt and is more easily pulled from your hands. Keep the balance of the longe line coiled in large loops in one hand. The other hand (near the colt's halter) should hold the line below the snap so that you don't inadvertently unsnap it.

Most colts react to the girth being tightened around their barrel. A surcingle is an easy way to prepare the colt for a saddle.

Approach the colt with the surcingle and let him see it and smell it before you place it on his back. If he has been handled and groomed, he should readily accept it. However, a colt that has spent two years in pasture may spook at an unfamiliar object. Lay the surcingle gently across his back. Be prepared for him to spook or jump when he feels the straps on the opposite side. Once you have the surcingle across his back, slide it slowly up and down and back and forth across his back. If the colt stands quietly, reach under and gently bring the end of the surcingle up so that you can buckle it. If the colt is nervous, continue to rub it up and down his back until he relaxes. *Never* put your face in a position where the colt could reach it if he kicks. Once you have the opposite end of the surcingle, buckle it *just snugly enough so that it stays in place and the colt can't get a foot caught under it.* For safety, it is best to get the surcingle buckled and then get out of the colt's way. If the colt reacts to the surcingle by bolting or rearing, hold the longe line and let him circle in a *large* circle around you. Be sure that you are in a safe place. (Most colts won't react until they are asked to longe, but do be careful.) He'll soon realize that the surcingle won't hurt him. When the colt settles down, you can gradually tighten the surcingle a little more if necessary.

Once the surcingle is tightened somewhat snugly around the colt's barrel, ask him to longe, using the longe line attached to his halter with a chain under his nose, if necessary. Stand on the side of the colt, never in front of him, in case he bucks or rears and goes over backwards. This doesn't happen often, but be prepared. If it does, don't make a big deal out of it or you'll teach him that lying down will end his lessons. Stay out of his way, *immediately* but calmly ask him to get up, then proceed.

Cluck to ask him to move forward. Let him move off at whatever gait he chooses. Don't overly enforce your cues to walk, jog, and lope at this point. Let him adjust to the feel of a girth around his barrel. Some colts will walk a few steps and then begin to buck. Others will squeal and race madly around the pen, and some will not react at all. Stay in the center of the pen, out of the colt's way, and let him learn that the surcingle won't hurt him nor will it come off. I don't punish a colt for bucking at this point. He's bucking because he's afraid. If you jerk on the longe line, you could hurt him, adding pain to his fear. But do make him stay in your longeing circle using a pull-and-release method.

He'll soon learn that the unfamiliar "monster" strapped to his back will not hurt him. Continue to longe him for five or ten minutes *after* he relaxes. This reinforces in his mind that there is nothing to be afraid of. Longe him with the surcingle for a week or two, then proceed to longeing with a saddle.

SADDLING

A colt can be longed with a light saddle before he is physically ready to be ridden. When you saddle a colt the first time, don't use a saddle pad unless the colt is quiet. You want to get the saddle on his back and cinched tightly enough so that it will not slip under his belly, and then you want to get out of his way. The first few times, it is easiest to have a knowledgeable helper hold the colt's head. He can control the movement of the colt while you put the saddle on the colt's back.

If a colt will not let you approach him with a saddle, place it in the middle of the round pen. Then turn him loose to investigate it for an hour or so, for as many days as necessary. This gives him the opportunity to find out for himself that it won't hurt him. He may sniff it, paw at it, or bite it, so use an old saddle. He should then allow you to approach him with it. If, after a week or so in the round pen, he will not stand to let you saddle him, stand him sideways about two feet away from a fence. Don't box him into a corner because his only way out will be through you. By standing him sideways against a fence, your helper can control the colt's forward or backward movement, and the fence helps to keep him straight.

If a colt is extremely nervous, tie the stirrups together over the top of the saddle prior to placing it on his back. This keeps the off stirrup from hitting his side when you gently place the

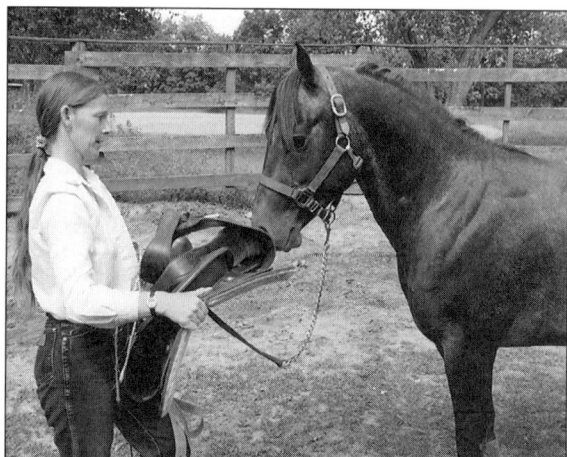

Let the colt sniff the saddle before you place it on his back.

Watch the colt's reaction when you place the saddle on his back the first time.

saddle on his back. It also keeps the stirrups from bumping his sides until you later untie them. On most colts this is not necessary, but it may be helpful on those few skittish ones.

Bring the saddle to the side of the colt's neck. Let him sniff it. Rub it up and down his neck, then on the left side of his back. If he stands reasonably quietly, gently place the saddle on his back. Most colts will stand quietly, but be prepared! If he leaps forward, lift it up and off his back. Don't let it fall to the ground! You will scare him and make it harder to saddle him the next time.

With a skittish colt, you can tie the stirrups together over the top of the saddle.

After the saddle is gently placed on his back, bring the end of the girth slowly and gently to your side. Run the strap through the ring of the girth and gently tighten it. Never jerk it tightly or you will later have a cinchy horse or one that fears being saddled because he was hurt. Again, be careful where you position your face. I try to do this step quickly in case the colt does act up. I want the saddle to be in place so that it can neither come off nor slip under his belly if he bolts or bucks. Never tighten a girth so much that it causes a colt extreme discomfort.

String girths seem to create sores more quickly on a colt than the fleece girths do.

BREAST COLLAR

A breast collar allows you to tighten the saddle somewhat less snugly. However, the first time a colt is saddled, I like to get the saddle on and get away from him for safety unless I've seen that the colt is accepting of new procedures. Most colts are fine, but again, play it safe. By the second day, the colt will usually accept being saddled and you'll have time to buckle the additional straps. A colt may still buck when you ask him to longe (some crow–hop for days), but most will usually not react badly when saddled. A breast collar is helpful on a colt that has "no" withers because it will keep the saddle in place. It is a judgment call as to whether you should use the breast collar the first or second day.

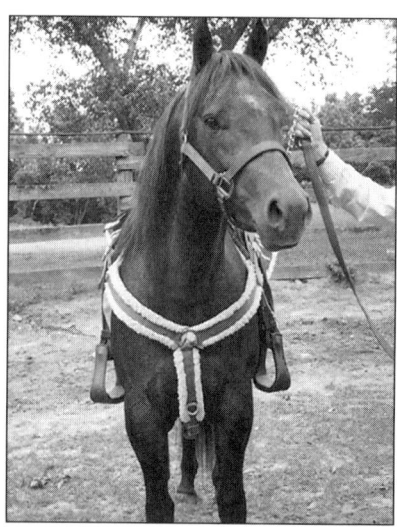

A breast collar is helpful in keeping your saddle in place on a round colt.

LONGEING

With the saddle in place and tightened enough so that it will not slip under his belly, longe the colt. The same rules apply as for longeing with the surcingle. Cluck to ask him to move off at whatever gait he prefers, and stay in a safe position. Longeing him will allow you to have control yet remain at a safe distance from him. After a day or two, when he relaxes while longeing with the saddle on his back, begin to ask him to obey your cues to walk, jog, or lope. Saddle the colt every time you longe him. It only takes a few minutes and prepares him for being ridden.

If your colt is really skittish, you can put the saddle on the first day without a pad (to longe him).

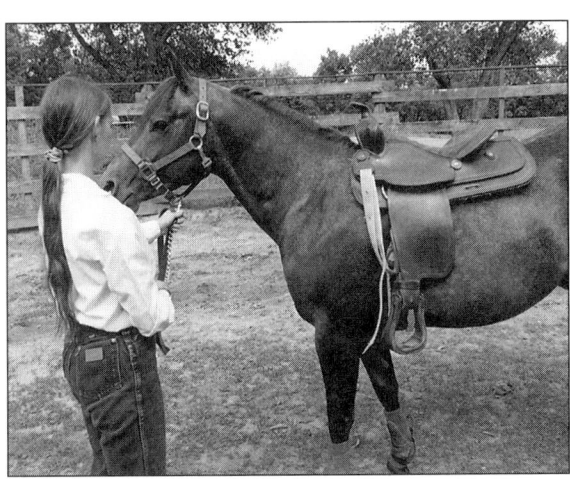

Although you may introduce him to a bit and bridle prior to saddling him, don't longe him the first week with a bit in his mouth. Always introduce new training procedures one at a time.

BITTING

Before you put a bit in a colt's mouth, check for wolf teeth—small pointed premolars located immediately in front of the upper molars. Wolf teeth can cause extreme discomfort and should be removed by your vet. To prepare a colt for bridling, slip your halter on and off over his ears rather than unbuckling the cheek strap. Later, when you bridle him, he shouldn't react badly to the headstall being slipped on or off over his ears in the same way.

His first bit should be an eggbutt snaffle, or other mild snaffle that fits comfortably in his mouth. The larger the mouthpiece, the milder the bit (if it fits the colt's mouth). This is an acceptable mild mouthpiece to ride with at a later time. To

*Use a bit that fits your colt. I prefer, the colt willing, to start with
the top eggbutt snaffle. Then I change to the D ring snaffle, middle,
which is slightly thinner and so slightly sharper.
I keep most colts in the bottom, sweet iron snaffle.
The chin strap keeps me from pulling the bit
through the colt's mouth, if I really need to
take hold of him and pull him around.*

introduce a bit to a colt, use a bridle with the reins removed. Adjust the bit so that there is a slight wrinkle in the corners of his lips. Let the bit hang in his mouth for an hour or so because he must learn to carry it. Repeat this lesson for a few days or a week or until he seems comfortable carrying the bit.

BRIDLING

Because I'm short, when I bridle a colt, I hold the headstall in my right hand over the colt's nose. That way, I can hold the colt's nose down as well and keep him from raising his head and avoiding the bit. A taller person can put his right hand between the colt's ears to accomplish the same thing. I use my left hand to hold the bit and ask the colt to open his mouth with my left thumb or finger against his tongue. Then I gently slide the bit into his mouth, being sure not to bump his teeth.

Removing the bit correctly is as important as putting it in correctly. Slip the headstall off over his ears and hold it up until the colt drops the bit out. Don't pull the bit out of his mouth— wait for the colt to "spit" it out. If you bang a colt's teeth with a

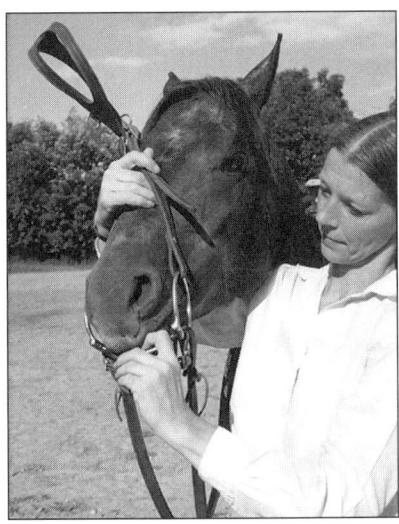

Hold your right hand over the colt's nose to keep his head down.

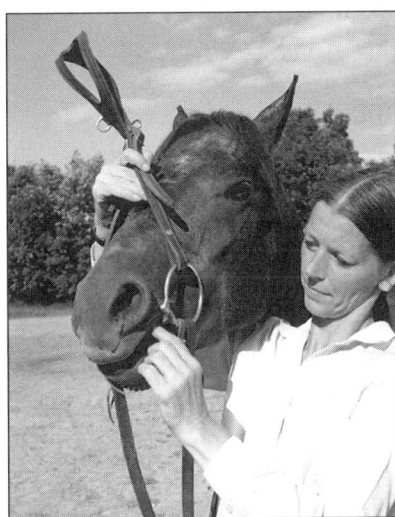

Ask the colt to open his mouth as you gently put the bit in.

Put his right ear in the head stall.

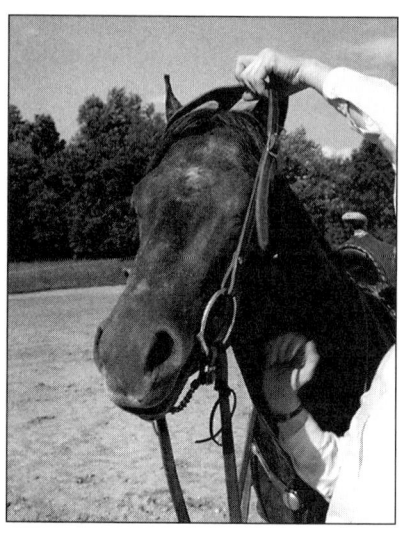

Then put his other ear in.

Let the colt spit the bit out so that you don't bump his teeth.

bit either when you put it in or take it out, he will learn that a bit causes pain and he will then try to avoid it. Start him correctly to avoid future problems.

Be prepared for the colt to let you put the bit into his mouth the first time or two without a problem because he has no idea what to expect. By the second or third time, he will begin to understand and may try to avoid being bitted, especially if you've banged his teeth. If a colt gives you problems, back him into a corner of a stall and spend as much time as necessary to get the bit into his mouth. *Stay calm.* This is training, not a fight. The colt has to learn that you *will* put the bit into his mouth. Stay to the side of him because he may rear. Put the bit into his mouth ten, twenty, even thirty times—as many as it takes for him to accept being bridled properly. End your lesson on a good note. Then come back an hour or two later and repeat the procedure.

Once a colt accepts the bit in his mouth, longe him with a halter over his bridle, with the longe line attached to the ring on the halter. This teaches him to carry the bit while moving without applying pressure to the bit. Let the colt learn to carry both the saddle and the bridle while longeing to prepare him for being ridden.

Next, you'll begin teaching the colt to "give" to bit pressure before you begin to teach him to ground drive.

CHAPTER SEVEN

Ground Driving

————————— ◆ —————————

Early training—longeing, saddling and bridling, and ground driving—is important because it lays the foundation for future training under saddle. Don't rush through these steps, especially if you have never started a colt before. A few extra days spent on each step will never harm a horse but rushing through will. Let the colt tell you when to advance to the next step by his acceptance of each previously taught step. In this way, you have a solid foundation on which to build. Teaching your colt to ground drive will teach him to obey your rein cues before you actually mount for the first time. Once your colt understands these rein cues *and* knows the specific cues to walk, jog, and lope while carrying both the saddle and the bridle on the longe line, the transition to following these same cues under saddle is an easy one.

Using a logical, step-by-step program mentally prepares a colt for being ridden. Also, as you work with a colt on the ground, notice how he reacts to certain training procedures. Evaluating him now will give you an idea of what to expect when you mount the first time and how the colt's future training may proceed. Your colt is learning what is acceptable behavior as he matures into an adult horse; his days of cavorting freely in the pasture are over. Make your colt respect your aids and cues now so that he will also respect them under saddle.

A colt should be started in a mild snaffle bit that fits him comfortably, or in a sidepull as described in Chapter 8. A large mouthpiece, such as a hollow mouth snaffle, is a good choice to use for starting a colt. However, if he cannot comfortably close his mouth with this bit in, try a somewhat smaller mouthpiece. Don't use a very thin mouthpiece because it is too severe. It is much like pulling on a thin wire in your hand, which cuts into it, as compared to pulling on a thick rope that only exerts pressure.

Before you actually begin ground driving the colt, spend a few minutes longeing him off the ring on his halter while he carries both the saddle and the bridle. When I first bridle a colt, I leave the halter on under the bridle. This is an easy way to keep control of the colt if he does not want to take the bit willingly.

After he settles down and is ready to work, snap the longe line to the ring on the side of the bit nearest to you. Ask the colt to longe. Once he begins to walk or jog around the longeing circle, pull the longe line to ask him to give (or turn) his head to you in response to the rein pressure on the bit. This is the beginning of teaching him to respect bit pressure. Don't pull so hard that his entire body turns. Only ask him to turn his head and neck slightly in toward you as he continues to follow the longeing circle. When he obeys and turns his head slightly toward you, release the pressure on the longe line immediately and let him straighten his head and continue to circle around you. This release of pressure rewards him and tells him that he responded correctly. This is the beginning of giving and turning in response to rein pressure.

TEACHING TO GIVE TO BIT PRESSURE

Teaching a colt to "give to the bit" is a process that continues throughout his training. You begin to teach a colt to give to pressure and to turn in response to a "pull" on the bit. Then, as you progress with his training, giving to the bit will teach him to flex at the poll and to carry his face (or head) in a vertical position. A horse that has been taught to give to the bit correctly will have what is called a "face" on him. He will not raise his head in the air to avoid the pressure. He will have been taught the proper response—that the way to gain release of the pressure is to flex at the poll or to "back off of bit pressure."

During these first few lessons, only ask him to bend or "give" his head occasionally—maybe once or twice during each circle. However, don't ask at the same place each time. By spacing your requests, you give him time to absorb the request (the pull), time to react to the pull (and to bend or give his head), and time to absorb the reward (the release of pressure on the bit). Asking too often can confuse a colt and make him think that he has done something wrong. He will think that he is being corrected for a wrong response by the constant pull on the lines.

ASK FIRST

Always ask lightly at first—the lightest amount of pressure that the colt will respond to. Only then should you increase the tension if the colt doesn't respond. Give him time—three seconds or so—to respond so that he may avoid the stronger aid or pull. Releasing the aid when he turns rewards him and tells him that he did as you asked. Over a period of days, the colt should begin to respond to a lighter aid or pull. You are laying the foundation of teaching a colt to respond to light aids which is the desired result of any training program.

If a colt ever begins to race around the circle or pulls on the longe line, whether it be with the line attached to a halter or to a bit, pull and release until he behaves appropriately. Anytime you pull on a colt, always gain contact first and then pull—never snatch or jerk. If you continuously pull as the colt circles around you, he will be able to pull against you and will probably win the battle if not the war. If you pull and release, he has nothing to pull against, giving you the advantage and hence the opportunity to teach him that he must respect and obey your cues.

TYING HIS HEAD SIDE TO SIDE

After he understands the concept of giving to pressure on the bit on the longe line, begin to tie his head first to one side and then the other. You'll need to attach a set of reins to the bridle to do this. Six-foot cotton lead lines work also. In a round pen or other enclosed area, tie one rein to the saddle horn long enough so that the colt has room to bend his head in the opposite direction. Bend his head *slightly* in the opposite direction with the other rein and tie that rein with a quick-release knot on the girth strap directly below the skirt of the saddle.

Tie the rein on the side on which you wish him to bend into the girth, right below the skirt of the saddle.

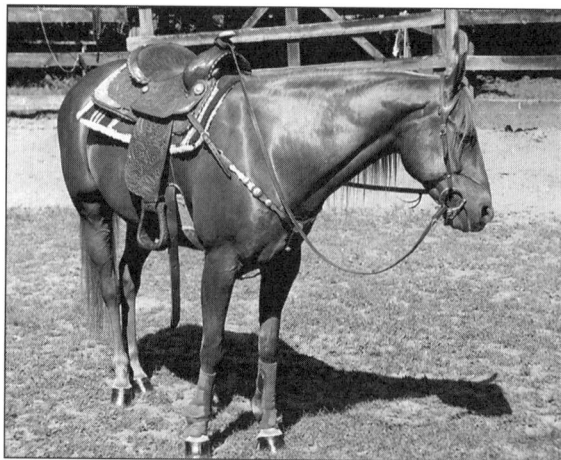

Tie the opposite rein loosely so that the horse has room to move his head freely.

For the first few days, tie his head slightly in each direction for five to ten minutes per side. Use only enough pressure so that the rein comes into contact with the bit when he tries to hold his head in a straightforward position. He may fight, but he must learn that his reward comes from giving to the bit and bending his head in the proper direction.

Over a period of days, gradually increase the amount of bend. If the colt moves as you are tying the rein, walk around the circle with him as you tie the rein. Then step out of the circle as you let or make the colt continue to circle. Stand out of the colt's way, but don't leave him unattended. Again, remember to use a quick-release knot for safety. The colt will learn this lesson more quickly if you ask him to continue circling at a walk rather than standing in one spot and lugging on the bit.

GROUND DRIVING

After a week or two of tying a colt on each side for ten to fifteen minutes at a time, you can begin to ground drive him. (Continue to tie a colt's head on each side for some time, incorporating the lessons in Chapter 9. This reinforces that he must give to the bit.) He now understands the procedure of turning his head in response to rein pressure and therefore should turn readily when you ground drive him.

I like to use a saddle when I ground drive a colt because it also prepares him for being ridden, but a surcingle is acceptable. Before attaching your long lines to the bit, tie the stirrups together under the colt's belly. A piece of baling twine works fine and is readily available and easily disposed of when you are finished with your ground-driving lessons. If you omit tying the stirrups, you will have no control over the colt because the stirrups will rise.

When you are ready to attach the long lines to the bit, keep either a longe line or lead line attached to the colt's halter so that he cannot walk off as you attach the driving lines. If you don't have driving lines, two cotton longe lines without chains work equally as well. Cotton will not burn your hands as nylon will.

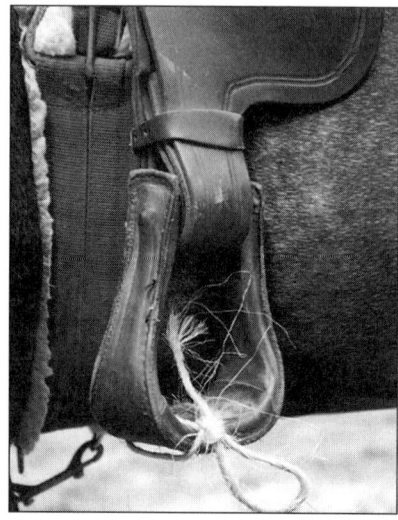

To ground drive a horse with a saddle, tie the stirrups together under the saddle. A piece of baling twine works well. This fleece girth is what I like to use, especially when starting colts.

ATTACH THE LINES

It is easiest to have a helper hold the colt while you attach the long lines or driving lines. If you are working alone, coil the long lines and keep them in one hand. Then run the line through the stirrup on the left side of the colt and attach it to his bit. Walk in front of the colt to the right side, holding the balance of the coiled lines in one hand. Bring the part of the second rein that buckles to the bit over his neck, then run it through the right stirrup to repeat the same procedure at the bit. With the coiled lines still in your hand, walk around to the front of the colt. You will now have both lines on the left side. By doing this, there is less chance of the colt being spooked by excess lines dangling, and it keeps the lines from dragging on the ground where the colt may step on them. Never let a colt step on any kind of rein because it can permanently damage his mouth.

After attaching the long driving lines, you can remove the longe line if you're working in a round pen. When I am working outside a pen on a spooky colt, I sometimes keep the longe line attached to his halter under the bridle. If he then tries to bolt, I can control him through the use of his halter rather than pulling on his bit. If it is too awkward handling so many lines, you can ask a helper to hold the longe line. Your assistant can keep the longe line attached to the colt's halter until the colt understands and responds to the long lines. Your helper should stay about ten feet away from the colt and only help to control the colt when necessary.

Otherwise, use your long lines to direct the colt. When the colt obeys your long-line cues, your helper can then unsnap his longe line.

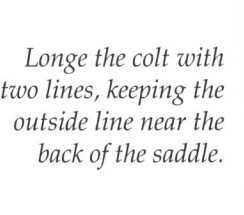

Longe the colt with two lines, keeping the outside line near the back of the saddle.

IN THE ROUND PEN

If you are working in a round pen, begin by asking the colt to longe in a circle to the left with the right rein laid over the saddle. He will stay in the circle because of the fence. Ask the colt to circle a few times or until he looks relaxed. Ask him to halt, using your verbal "Whoa!" command that you taught him on the longe line. (He won't yet understand a rein cue.) Walk up to the left side of the colt and place the right rein behind the cantle of the saddle. Lengthening your reins, move far enough away from the colt that if he decides to spook, he will not jump into you when you slide the right rein into position to ground drive him. Most colts are not used to feeling ropes on their hindquarters and may leap forward or kick. Stay to the side for safety. Once you are far enough away from the colt so that he

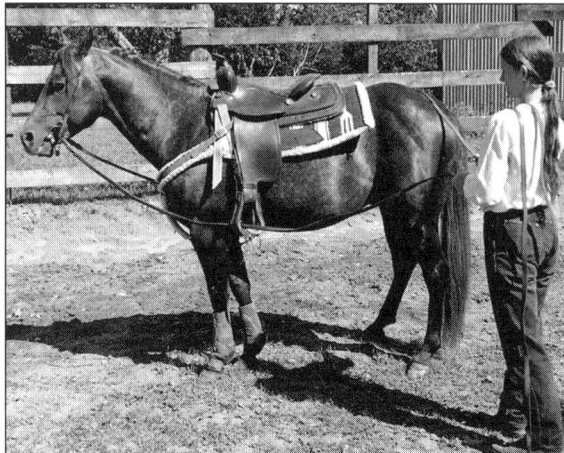

Slide the outside rein slowly and gently over the colt's rump and into place. Be prepared. Some colts will spook when feeling the line.

can't reach you if he kicks, gently slide the rein down the right side of his rump, keeping the lines above his hocks so that he doesn't become tangled in them. Once you have brought the reins into the proper driving position, stay slightly to the inside of your circle and ask the colt to walk forward. Be prepared—he may jog because he is frightened of the rope above his hocks. Talk to him in a soothing voice, and unless he is racing madly, let him jog until he settles.

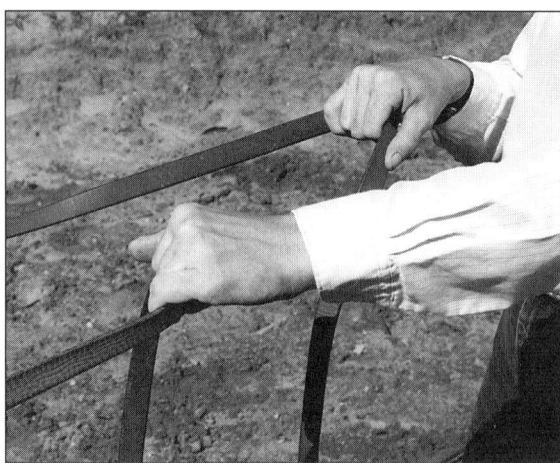

Remember that to ask the colt to turn to the right, you must loosen the left rein, allowing him the freedom to turn his head.

THE SPOOKY COLT

Using a round pen is helpful, especially in the case of a spooky colt. He covers a greater distance on the rail while you can stay to the inside of the circle and thus be able to keep up with him. Let him jog until he settles. If he begins to bolt, quickly turn his nose into the fence, which will stop him. Don't pull back on the reins to stop him because he has not yet been taught to stop with that signal. You don't want to hurt him or scare him any more than he already is. After he stops, talk quietly to him as you give him time to realize that he wasn't hurt by this new experience. Most colts that bolt forward when they first feel the long line behind them will soon learn to accept this new training procedure.

Once he seems somewhat relaxed, ask him to walk forward a few feet and stop, using the verbal "Whoa!" that you taught him on the longe line. This is one of the times when teaching a colt to respect the whoa cue will come in handy. The other time is when you ride the first few days. Don't forget to teach that "Whoa!" means to stop and stand *now!* Verbally praise him when he does stop and repeat walking forward a few steps and stopping. Then ask him to walk a greater distance before stopping.

TEACHING THE CUES

Once the colt relaxes with the feel of the lines on his body, begin to teach him the rein cues to turn and to halt. Your position can now be slightly to the inside behind him, still out of kicking distance.

Keep equally light contact on each rein as you ask him to walk forward. When you ask him to turn to the left, put more tension on the left rein as you move your right hand forward to continue to keep equal contact. Think of the reins as bicycle handlebars. When one hand moves back to pull, the other must move forward to give enough rein to allow the colt to turn his head. This is very important. Not only must you do this when you ground drive a colt, you must remember the bicycle handlebars when you ride him. Using this method, you can keep the colt between the reins.

TURNING

As the colt is walking forward, ask him to make a large circle to the left. Cut the pen short if you are in a round pen. In the beginning, if a colt doesn't respond to a light pull, increase the tension on the line until he does turn. He must learn that he has to turn when you signal with your reins to turn. When he does turn, reward him by release of pressure.

The first few times, especially if you are new at this, the colt may make a sharp turn. You'll need to move quickly to keep your position behind him. Ask more lightly the next time so that he doesn't overbend. When the colt understands the concept of turning in response to rein pressure, begin to use lighter and lighter pressure to ask him to turn. This teaches him to respond to a light signal. After asking him to make three or four circles to the left, repeat the process to the right. After he understands to turn, begin to make figure-eights and serpentines. A colt must learn something first on one side and then on the other side because his brain doesn't connect as ours does. Working first one side and then the other helps the colt so that he doesn't have to "change his mind" from side to side initially.

Your goal, the end result of any training program, is using the reins as a signal to tell him to turn, *not* a way to *force* him to turn.

Ask the colt to cross the pen, being sure to turn both left and right.

"WHOA!"

Near the end of your lesson, begin to teach him to halt. Say "Whoa!" first, then lightly increase the tension on both reins and hold them. Don't pull back! You want to create a barrier for the colt to walk into—you do not want to pull him back. The first couple of times, hold the lines until he comes to a complete halt. As soon as he stops all forward motion, release the pressure on the lines. If he takes a step forward, repeat the same procedure, again releasing as soon as he stops. After a few days, begin to release the pressure as soon as he *begins* to halt. This teaches him that he is rewarded for responding to a light *signal* to halt. Then ask him to walk forward halfway around the pen and ask him to halt again. End your lesson when he has performed a request to the best of his ability or has shown a slight improvement from the beginning of your lesson. Always end your lesson on a good note, not when the colt is fighting you.

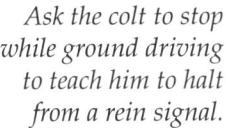

Ask the colt to stop while ground driving to teach him to halt from a rein signal.

TO REMOVE THE LINES

To remove the lines, walk to the side of the colt to his shoulder as you hold the lines up so that he will not step on them. Snap a lead line or longe line to the colt's halter. Unbuckle the right line and run it back through the stirrup. Place it either on the ground or over the saddle. Walk in front of the colt and unbuckle the left line. Once both lines are through the stirrups, you can place the lines on the ground and walk the colt forward. Then, depending on the colt, either turn the colt so that he is facing the driving lines and coil the lines, or come back later to pick up the lines after you put the colt away if he is somewhat spooky or skittish.

Continue to ground drive a colt for ten to twenty minutes a day until he will turn easily to the left or right and will go forward and halt on command. Some colts may accomplish this lesson in two days; others may take two weeks or more. Continue ground driving until you feel comfortable with the colt's response. After being taught to lighten up in response to bit pressure (discussed in the next chapter), his next lesson is to be mounted and ridden for the first time once he is of an age to ride. Having been taught to ground drive, the colt should now respond to the rein cues when he is mounted and should turn left or right or halt. From longeing, he has learned to walk, jog or trot, and canter or lope on command. By following this logical training program, a colt should be mentally prepared to be ridden. He should accept a rider on his back as just one more day of training.

The Sidepull

———————— ◆ ————————

The sidepull is a training device similar to a bosal or hackamore—it is a type of bridle without a bit. A sidepull can be used for initial training on a young horse or it can be used on an older horse that for various reasons will not or is unable to carry a bit. It is an effective training device to use when starting a young horse, especially if you are unsure of your hands or ability. When using a sidepull, you will not damage the bars of a colt's mouth because the pressure is on his nose. If your hands and seat (or ability) are not quite as far along as you'd like them to be, then using a sidepull for those initial rides may be just the ticket for you. A colt may stay in a sidepull indefinitely unless you plan to show him. In that case, check the showing rules and regulations in your chosen discipline.

A colt should respond well to a sidepull if he responds readily when you lead him and stop him from the ground with a halter and lead line. It is important to remember that a horse does not stop because a bit forces him to stop. He stops because he is obeying a signal from the bit and because he expects to get rewarded by the release of pressure when he does stop. Just as you can deaden a horse's mouth to the signals of a bit by using a prolonged cue or one that is too harsh, you can also deaden a horse's response to signals from a sidepull. A sidepull should be used with a pull-and-release method. Use little tugs that become sharper, if necessary, on the reins, rather than a straight-back or sideways pull. Anytime you get into a pulling contest with a horse, the horse is sure to win because of his superior size and strength. You must outthink him. By using a pull-and-release method, the horse has nothing to set against and therefore cannot outpull you.

The noseband of a sidepull is a stiff, round nosepiece about the diameter of a penny. It is sometimes made of a coarse, rigid rope, a stiff nylon rope, or a braided leather over a stiff inner core. It is similar to a bosal except that the reins of the sidepull are attached to rings on the side rather than on the bottom. Attached to these same rings is a chin strap that runs under the

The sidepull is a form of bridle without a bit.

horse's nose. The chin strap does not add pressure under the horse's jaw as it does with a shank or leverage-type bit. It is mainly used to keep the sidepull in place.

ADJUSTING THE SIDEPULL

The proper way to adjust a sidepull is to place the noseband right above the point of the horse's nose where bone meets the cartilage. This is about halfway between his nostril and cheekbone. You will feel the bone end if you run your hand down the front of a horse's face. Right below the point where the sidepull should be positioned, you will feel the hard bone change to cartilage.

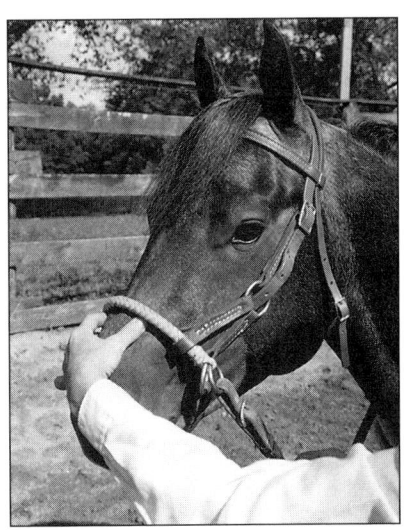

Feel down the colt's nose to where the bone meets the cartilage. This is about halfway between his nostrils and cheekbone.

Most sidepulls are sold without reins. You must either attach your own reins or purchase them separately. Cotton lead lines are a quick and inexpensive choice if you do not have a spare set of reins. Cotton lead ropes are thick and will not burn your hands as nylon will if the horse should pull. The snaps on the ends also make a quick and easy way to attach the reins, and the lead ropes can be put back into use as lead lines when you are done using the sidepull.

A properly adjusted sidepull.

SINGLE OR DOUBLE

A sidepull comes either single or double, the double being the more severe of the two. The double sidepull has two matching nosebands that lie side by side across the horse's nose. To start a young horse, use the single sidepull. The double sidepull may be effective on an older horse that doesn't respond well to a single sidepull, since it is more severe, but it is too harsh to use in starting a colt. Teaching a colt to enjoy being ridden is one of your first goals when you start him under saddle and inflicting excessive pain will only cause a colt to fear being ridden, thus defeating your purpose. Using equipment that is too harsh can sour a colt on being ridden for life.

As with any new training equipment, it is more cost effective to first borrow it if possible. In this way, you'll have the opportunity to try it on your horse to see if it is effective. This way, you will not have to purchase an item that you may only use for a brief time.

THE HALF-BREED SIDEPULL

A half-breed sidepull is the same type of headstall/noseband combination but with a snaffle bit attached to the sidepull noseband. On this type of sidepull, the reins attach to the snaffle bit and noseband. With a half-breed sidepull, your horse feels the pressure from the bit as well as from the rigid noseband. The half-breed sidepull can be used as a training step between a sidepull and a bit alone. It is not necessary to use this step, but some people are more comfortable changing from a sidepull to a bit in this way. I mention it only to inform you that this option is available. You must find what works best for your colt. On the same note, you may decide that you'd rather not switch to a bit and may want to keep your colt in the sidepull indefinitely. Just remember that if you plan to show, a sidepull may not be acceptable equipment. Check the rules before entering.

RIDING IN THE SIDEPULL

When you begin to ride your colt in a sidepull, do not try to outpull him. You cannot force a colt to stop by pressure on his nose. To tell your colt to stop, first use the verbal whoa command that your colt learned on the longe line, followed by a "pull" on the reins, releasing as soon as he does stop. If your colt respects the whoa command from the ground, he should stop easily when you use this command from a mounted position followed by your giving a sidepull rein command. Give a light pull on the reins, then repeat the same pull and release

If the colt won't stop, guide him into the fence.

only a little more sharply if he didn't respond to the first command. If he still hasn't responded, use quick, short, sharp tugs on your reins. If he ignores that cue, pull his head into the fence and let the fence stop him. Don't let a colt learn now that he can ignore or disobey your cues.

RELEASE PRESSURE

Because you *immediately* release pressure as soon as a colt does stop, he soon learns that he is rewarded for stopping by release of all pressure. He will continue to stop to get the reward of release of pressure. However, if you keep pulling after he stops, he will never understand that he will be rewarded by release of pressure when he does stop. Pulling excessively, especially after a colt stops, will teach the colt to toss his head to evade the pain, to raise his head in the air to try to get away from the pressure, or to lower his head to try to pull the reins out of your hands.

Your hands should react by softening or releasing as soon as you feel a correct response. This is something that you should work on continually throughout your lifetime of riding horses. Releasing pressure as soon as a colt responds will teach him to respond to the light aid, showing him that he can avoid the harsher or prolonged aid. A colt learns to respond sooner once he understands that he is rewarded by the release of all pressure when he performs as you ask.

The same is true of turning. To ask your colt to turn to the left, initially bring your left direct rein hand to the outside, six to eight inches from the left side of his neck, and use the same pull-and-release method. If he doesn't respond, use quick tugs and releases. This will teach the colt that it is easier to give in (and turn) than to try to outpull you. Never give him a chance to pull on the rein and win and therefore learn that he can outpull you.

A horse's face can become bruised or even made raw from using a sidepull too harshly. Begin with a light cue and progress from there. Remember, however, that your safety always comes

To turn to the left, bring the left direct rein hand to the outside.

first. If a horse is reacting badly or putting you in an unsafe position, use as much pressure as necessary to get your point across. Keep yourself safe. If you must resort to using a harsh cue, and you release the pressure as soon as he gives in and behaves, all but the really untrainable horses will behave much better on the following day. You will have shown him that it is in his best interest to obey your cues. As much as we'd all like to be nice to our horses, there are times when they must be taught to respect and perhaps to fear—just a little—our commands, whether they come from a bit, a lead line, or a sidepull.

When the colt is responding properly, leave him alone. Release all aids and sit quietly.

If you want to start a young horse without fear of hurting his mouth, a sidepull may be just the answer. But no matter what you start a baby in, he must learn to understand and then respect these new mounted cues. By always rewarding a correct response on his part with release of pressure, he will soon learn that he is rewarded for performing as you ask. Always give your cues in the same, consistent manner and reward him consistently as well. Only by repeating your corrections and rewards can he learn what is expected of him.

Some horses will learn to respond easily to a sidepull and some will not. Use your own judgment. It is best to always begin training in a small enclosed area. In this way, if a colt bolts or spooks, he is confined within the fence or enclosure. Only when your colt has shown you, consistently, that he will perform as you request, should you progress to bigger areas, such as a fenced pasture and then finally to the wide open trails. "Listen" carefully to what your colt is telling you before you advance to the next area. If he will not respond to a sidepull in a small arena, do not expect him to respond to a sidepull in a bigger area. Either spend the additional time in a small enclosed area teaching him that he must listen to your commands, or switch to a different type of headgear that he will respond to.

Teaching Your Colt to Accept Bit Pressure

◆

The colt began to learn the meaning of bit pressure and how to respond to it when he learned how to ground drive. He also learned to longe and accepted carrying a bit and bridle. The colt was longed with the line attached to the bit and his head was "pulled" to you, asking him to turn his head in response to rein pressure. When he "gave" you his head, or turned his head to you in response to a pull on the line, he was rewarded by the release of pressure. The next step, explained in the chapter on ground driving, was to tie his head side to side, again teaching him to give to pressure to reward himself.

After a colt gives readily when tied side to side, the next step may be accomplished in one of two ways. You may tie a rein, one on each side, to the girth where the skirt of the saddle ends. This is the same place where you tied the single rein to teach the horse to give to pressure side to side. The alternative method is to use a running martingale.

A running martingale has two rings (attached to the opposite end of the strap that attaches to the girth), rather than just the one strap (which attaches to the noseband) as you would find on a standing martingale.

You can tie a rein to either side, as shown. This colt's head is exactly vertical, the maximum to set one at.

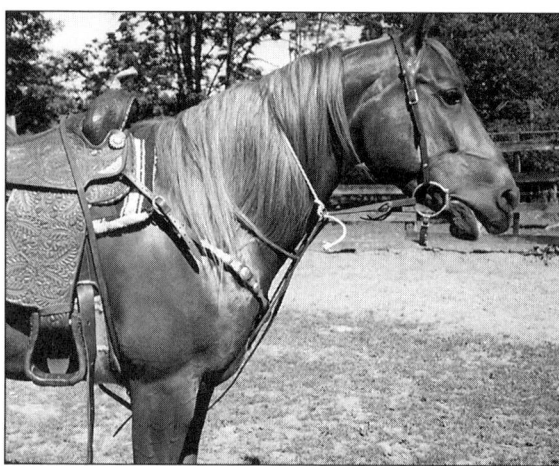

This is my preferred way to bit a colt with a running martingale. If a colt ever sticks his nose in the air, like this, and starts to run backwards, you must immediately send him forward.

You'll need eight-foot reins attached to a snaffle bit if you choose to use the running martingale. The running martingale is my preference. You may *only* use some sort of snaffle bit—a bit with no shanks. (Using either of these methods with the reins attached to the shank on a bit would put excessive pressure on the colt's mouth.)

RUNNING MARTINGALE

With a running martingale, adjust and then tie the rings so that when the reins are attached to the bit, through the rings, they make a straight line to the saddle horn, even though they drop between the horse's front legs. To hold the rings in place, take a piece of twine or a strap and tie one end to one ring. Put the twine over the horse's neck and tie it to the other ring, holding the rings in the same position they will be in when you hold them while mounted. Run the reins through the rings of the running martingale, go down between the horse's front legs, then tie the reins together up over the top of the saddle, behind the horse's front legs.

START LOOSELY

The first couple of days are the most crucial. Start very loosely, using only enough pressure on the reins so that if the horse sticks his nose in the air, he'll feel light pressure. Do not start a colt too tightly. He needs time to learn that the proper response is to drop his head to a vertical position or to flex at the poll to gain relief from bit pressure. This is not something that you can rush any horse through. Over a period of days, you'll see the colt hitting the bit and dropping his nose (bringing it back) in response to the pressure on the bit. Then you may tighten the reins a little every few days. Tying a horse too tightly initially can easily cause him to panic and flip over backwards. Be sure to start loosely!

Once the colt learns that the way to gain relief from pressure is to back off of the bit, he will flex at the poll, as shown.

Initially, the colt may stick his nose in the air until he learns to give to pressure.

Here his head is beginning to come down.

Once the colt's head is set in this way, you may either free longe him or use a longe line attached to his halter or a longeing cavesson. Ask the colt to move off in a longeing circle. The first time or two that he hits the bit, his head may come up and his hind end drop. He may try to stop and run backwards. In the worst scenario, he may rear and go over backwards. Use your longe whip, extended away from you so that you stay out of harm's way, and send the horse forward with the whip. Do this aggressively enough so that the colt goes forward. Don't let him start running backwards. *Make him go forward* so that he'll realize the way to release all pressure on his mouth is to drop his nose and go forward.

KNOW YOUR COLT

Know your colt. If he fights every little thing that you do, start very loosely and very gradually tighten the pressure. If he's a calm, accepting type of colt, you can increase the pressure a little sooner, but *only after a few days of being tied very loosely.*

Once the colt is going around your longeing circle, ask him to walk, jog/trot, or lope/canter. You may ask him to halt and then repeat the process. Transitions are helpful to teach the colt that his nose must stay vertical even when he changes pace. However, changing gaits too often or too quickly will confuse a colt. Let him change gaits and then go at least twice around the circle (in a round pen) before you ask for another transition. This gives the colt time to realize that he performed as you asked and time to learn to give to bit pressure and to reward himself.

INCREASE TENSION ON THE REINS SLOWLY

Once you see the colt's nose drop to a vertical position every time he hits the bit, you can begin to tighten up the reins a little more—until his face is vertical. Never tie one so tightly

Until finally, his head comes down and he flexes at the poll. You can see the slight loop in the reins, showing there is no tension on the reins.

that his face is past vertical. That will teach him to overflex. He'll then learn to tuck his nose into his chest and go behind the bit, leaving you with no control at all.

Continue to longe the colt this way for ten to twenty minutes, four or five times a week, before you ride. It usually takes about three months (very possibly more) for a colt to really understand what you are asking—to give to the bit or to drop his nose to a vertical position in response to bit pressure. This is called putting a "face" on a horse. You don't have to ride the colt every day. Longeing him with his head tied in this way will accomplish a lot, even without riding. Never let the colt stop when he is fighting the bit while being longed. Wait until he is flexing properly, or to the best of his ability at that time. Then say "Whoa," let the colt stop, and untie his head. Spend a few minutes letting him relax and catch his wind, and either ride him or put him away for the day.

RIDING THE COLT

After the colt seems to understand, begin to ask him to give to the bit while you are riding him. To accomplish this, let the colt walk or jog along the rail. It is easier for a colt to learn this at the jog or trot as he naturally carries his head in a more vertical position. Once he's jogging or trotting, pick up light contact and take a light, even hold of the reins. Ask the colt to "give" his head to you and flex at the poll. Hold your hands steady. Do not pull back on the reins. As you take hold of his face (or the reins), you have to push or squeeze the colt up into the bridle with your legs.

Having control of a colt's head is only half of the procedure. You must push the colt's hindquarters up underneath him. Teaching him to first give his head to bit pressure while on the ground helps the colt to understand what you want *by the rein pressure only.* Pushing him into the bridle with your legs rounds the colt's back, making him travel in a frame. A colt cannot use himself properly, collect, or be physically prepared for the next maneuver if his hind end is strung out behind him. Rein pressure alone only tells a colt to stop and in no way helps a colt to travel better. Use your legs and make the colt use himself.

As soon as he "gives"—or drops his nose to a vertical position—and rounds his back, release the rein pressure and let him continue to move forward. You can verbally praise him the first few times to help him understand that he did the right thing.

Rather than looking to see if the colt's head is flexed at the poll, you only need to feel with your hands. If your hands stayed steady in the same place, as they should have, you'll no longer feel any "pull" or pressure on the reins. The colt will feel "soft" in your hands.

As you continue with this exercise, only ask the colt to give or flex for a brief moment off and on throughout your schooling session. Over time, as he understands, gradually ask him to hold the flexed position for longer periods of time. Don't overdo it. Don't ask him to hold that position for long sessions, and don't ask him over and over again without rewarding him by a rest or a relaxing walk or trot on a long rein. Gradually asking him to extend the time that he holds the flexed position will let the colt understand, and his muscles will also develop properly.

When you feel the colt soften in your hands, release the pressure to reward him. Reward the colt by releasing pressure every time that he gives to you. You "give" the colt back his "face" every time that he "gives" it to you. You slowly, over weeks, ask him to hold that position longer.

An untrained colt will stick his nose in the air to avoid bit pressure. An untrained colt (or horse) puts his nose in the air to put the bit pressure on the corners of his mouth or lips. Bit pressure hurts less on the corners of a horse's mouth than on the bars of his mouth. An untrained horse will try to avoid pain in the best way that he knows. By teaching a horse to "give" to pressure, or drop his nose to a vertical position, he learns through months of repetition that the proper response—the proper way to gain relief from pressure—is to flex at the poll and give his face.

Teaching a colt to give to the bit, and keeping him trained to do so, requires that you have good hands and that you don't abuse the horse's mouth. The goal of any training procedure is to have a horse that responds to light, barely seen aids. Abusing a colt's mouth by pulling too hard, too often, or for unnecessary reasons will set your training back—possibly by months. You must constantly be aware of what your hands are doing so that the colt will continue to improve.

A horse that flexes at the poll and gives to the bit, remaining soft and light in your hand, will not fight you. Almost always before a horse leaps sideways, tries to run through the bridle, or does any number of other evasive tactics, he will stick his nose in the air. If the horse keeps his head flexed, staying soft, he is willing to listen and to do as you ask. "Once you have a horse's face, you have control of his mind."

GIVING TO THE BIT

After training a colt to give to the bit through the use of a snaffle as mentioned earlier, you may ride this colt in a shank bit. A bit is only as strong as the hands that use it. I will sometimes put a horse in a somewhat stronger bit so that he respects the signals given by the bit. I don't use a stronger bit so that I can pull harder—I use a stronger bit so that I can become lighter, or use less of a "pull" with a horse. But until a colt is trained to the signals of a bit, I stay with a snaffle (or with the lightest bit that the colt will "listen" to).

If you have a colt that does not listen with the bit you are using—and hopefully you have not abused his mouth by having heavy hands—try another bit. It does not always have to be stronger. Sometimes using just another type of bit will suffice. This exercise on bitting a horse must be done with some type of snaffle. But you are while riding a horse, you may try different types of bits. Your safety is always the first concern.

When starting a colt, you may find that he is unhappy in a certain type of bit. I start most of my colts in a hollow-mouth snaffle for a month or so, then I move on to a thinner, sweet iron

*Right:
Setting the colt's
head using a running
martingale.*

*Below:
Experiment with
different bits until
you find what your
colt works best in,
but always start with
a snaffle.*

snaffle. After training a colt in a snaffle, and putting a face on him, you may go on to a Mullen mouth bit, a low port, a straight bar, one with shanks that swivel or move independently from one another, or a solid medium port bit. Find which bit your colt likes and which bit he will perform the best in.

See if your colt can carry the bit comfortably. Does he have a fat tongue? He may need a bit with a higher port, giving him some tongue relief. Does he chew or fuss with the bit at a standstill before you even get on his back? Has he been this way right from the start? Did you check for wolf teeth or sharp edges that may be causing him pain?

Every horse is different. Some horses are born with snaffle mouths and they will listen in that type of bit forever. Other horses, born that way, are "toughened" by riders with heavy hands. A horse's mouth will become callused or the nerves deadened (just as your hands become callused and toughened by too much use) if too heavy of a hand is used on the reins too often. If you think that your hands are too heavy on the reins, take a few lessons on an older horse and work on teaching yourself to lighten up before you begin to train your colt to be light. You must try to find a bit that your colt works well in and one that he carries comfortably. As you continue to ride this colt, you may find that you need to change the type of bit to get the desired response. Don't be afraid to change bits. Experiment. Just be sure that it is not *your hands* that are at fault. Remember that this cold piece of steel is in the horse's *mouth*.

If your colt won't listen in the bit that you are using, go to a somewhat stronger bit. Never sacrifice your safety. A colt must learn to obey the signals given by a bit. Going to a stronger bit, if you have good hands and don't abuse a colt's mouth, can actually make a colt become lighter.

CHAPTER TEN

Mounting and Dismounting

———————— ◆ ————————

Many people take mounting a horse for granted, thinking nothing more of it than a way to get on a horse's back. However, there is a proper way to mount and as well as a proper way to dismount. Improper mounting can cause a series of problems, especially on a young horse. "Climbing" or "scrambling" up into the saddle can sour a colt on being mounted, as can sticking your toe into his girth area. Dropping your weight (improperly) into the saddle can hurt a colt's back, much as it would if a large child jumped onto your back for a piggyback ride. A colt will begin to move away to avoid being mounted because of the pain or discomfort that he associates with being mounted. Then, later, as he finds that he can make it difficult for you to mount (by moving away), he learns an easy way out of being ridden, at least temporarily. Because of a rider's error, the colt is now blamed for his lack of willingness or lack of training. Vices can be set into motion by a few incidents.

BEFORE YOU MOUNT FOR THE FIRST TIME

Before actually mounting a young colt for the first time, slap the stirrups against his sides. Tap on the seat of the saddle with your hand to prepare the colt for when you do mount. If

Tap the top of the saddle with your hand.

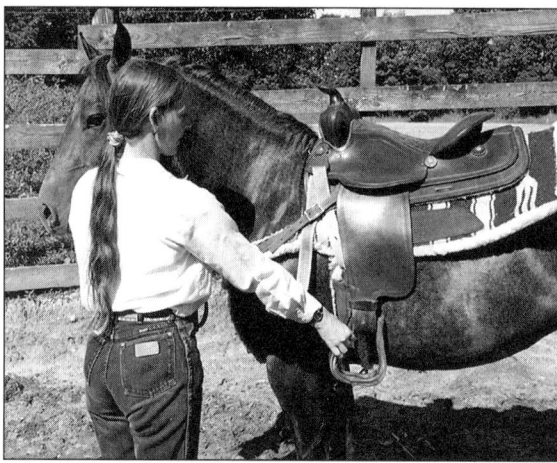

Flap the stirrups against the colt's sides.

the colt accepts this, and he should, then ask your assistant to hold the colt's head. Put just your toe into the stirrup. It is easier to remove just your toe than your entire foot if a quick dismount becomes necessary. Stand up in the stirrup. Place your weight across the saddle but do not physically get in the saddle yet. In this way, you can get to the ground easily if the colt really acts up. If he moves a few steps in either direction, you must stay with him to let him know that you will go through with this step.

Hold your reins with just enough tension so that the colt cannot walk forward.

Lay your weight over the saddle.

Once you are standing in the stirrup, run your hand up and down his neck on the off (right) side. Rub his sides. Then bring your hand down to the point where your leg will be. Rub and tap his side until he accepts that, then dismount. Repeat the entire standing-in-the stirrup process three or four more times. Repeat this for four or five days, usually at the end of your longeing or ground-driving lessons. When the time comes to actually mount, you will have already covered this step.

Rub your hand on the colt's off (right) side.

When I am ready to mount a colt for the first time and physically get into the saddle, I ask an assistant to hold the colt with one hand, using a cotton lead line so that it won't burn his hand if the colt pulls. I ask him to make a fist with the other hand and extend his arm straight out, pushing his fist into the colt's neck. In this way, if the colt acts up, or jumps sideways into my assistant, his straight arm will push him safely away from the horse. This straight arm will keep him the same distance (an arm's length) away from the horse at all times. This can keep an assistant from getting a toe stepped on or possibly getting knocked to the ground.

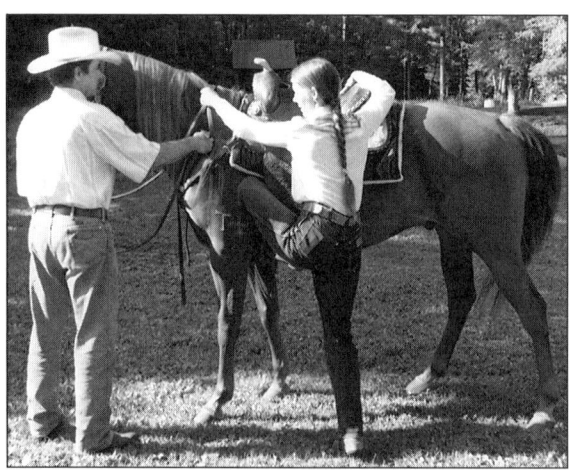

Ask your assistant to make a fist and push his arm into the colt's side. The colt should be set up reasonably square. This colt took a step as we snapped the photo.

DON'T STAND STILL FOR TOO LONG—YET

I never ask a colt to stand still for a long period of time when I get on the first time. If the colt is standing quietly, I spend a few minutes talking and moving slightly in the saddle to let the colt know that I am up there. If the colt is anxious to move, I continue to talk in a soothing voice but let him move off in the small circles at a walk. Mounting and riding for the first time is explained in more detail in Chapter 11.

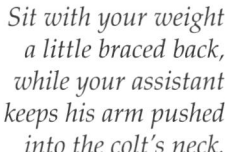

Sit with your weight a little braced back, while your assistant keeps his arm pushed into the colt's neck.

TEACHING THE COLT TO STAND FOR MOUNTING

Keep in mind that after your colt accepts being ridden, he should stand still for mounting. I start to enforce that the colt stand for mounting usually within five or six rides, sometimes later on a spooky colt and sooner on a quieter colt.

Teaching a colt the right way, shortly after he is comfortable with being mounted and being ridden, will save you from having problems later.

To mount a colt properly, be sure that he is standing squarely. Each of his four feet should be in a position resembling the four corners of a house. Try this yourself. If you stand with your two feet side by side, you most likely will not be pulled off balance to one side or the other. However, if your feet are placed one in front of the other, you can easily be pulled to one side or the other. The same is true of a horse, especially a young horse that has not yet learned to accommodate the slight sideways shift of the saddle and your weight as you mount.

STAND HIM UP SQUARE

To teach your colt to stand in one place with his legs squarely underneath him, first set one hind leg in position. Then, with your lead rope, ask the colt to move either forward or backward until the other hind leg sets up next up to the first hind leg. Once both hind feet are square, use your toe or your hand to place the remaining front leg in position. As soon as the colt is in position, say "Stand!" in a firm voice. You must say it as a command, not as a question. Horses respect authority. Make your voice sound like an army sergeant issuing orders and you'll get a quicker response.

USE THE WORD "STAND"

I use the word "stand" to tell the colt to "hold" or stand motionless in that position. I use the word "stand" rather than "whoa" to avoid confusion. I keep the word "whoa" for a complete stop and stand, whether mounted or on the ground. Horses can be taught simple word commands if a word is used consistently and enforced. You may feel more comfortable with the word "stay" or "wait." The word itself doesn't matter as long as it is consistent. I don't like to use the word "no" because it sounds too much like "whoa" and can cause confusion in a colt.

If you have a high-strung colt or one that does not like to stand in place for long periods of time, begin by asking him to stand still for ten to twenty seconds, then quickly praise him. He must understand that he only moves forward when you tell him to do so. Be sure that the colt doesn't get away with taking tiny steps forward. He may then think that he can choose the time to move forward. Many horses will begin to take tiny baby steps that lead to big steps. Teach the colt that *you* choose the time to move forward, not him.

LENGTHEN THE TIME THAT HE STANDS

Gradually increase the length of time that you ask a colt to stand still in a square position. Praise him verbally and/or by a scratch on his neck only when he does stand still. If he takes a step before you've asked him to move, put him right back in place, followed by praise when he does stand. This will show him what you want. If he needs a stronger correction, a prompt snap on the lead line combined with putting him back into place should help. Remember that to effectively show a colt what you want (or don't want), the correction or praise must be within three seconds. If you wait any longer than that, the colt will have no idea what you are correcting or rewarding him for.

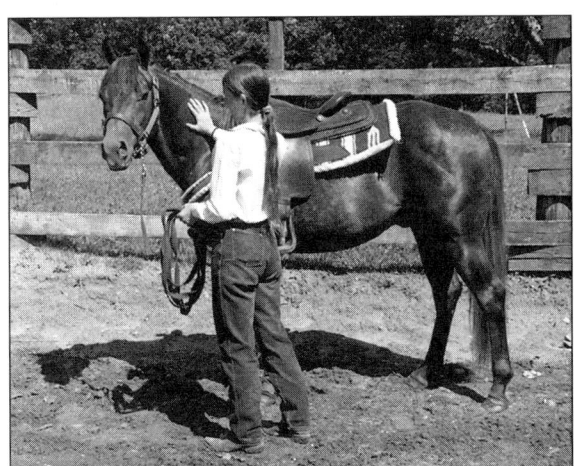

Praise your horse.

STAND TO MOUNT

Once your colt knows a verbal command to stand squarely, it is time to begin to teach him to stand squarely and still while you mount. If you use a mounting block, include standing still alongside the mounting block while you are training your colt to stand.

Mounting blocks are perfectly acceptable and are often-times beneficial, especially if you have a tall colt or you are not as nimble as you once were, having lost the "spring" from your step as you swing up into the saddle. Mounting problems can also be caused by people who, for one reason or another, try to "climb" up the side of the colt instead of stepping nimbly up into the saddle. Climbing up the side of the colt will pull the saddle off to one side as you struggle into it. This creates uncomfortable and improper pressure on the saddle. If you are not agile, or are uncomfortable mounting from the ground, use a mounting block—it can be beneficial to both you and your horse.

To actually mount, put both reins in your left hand, with enough slack so that you are not pulling on the reins and telling the colt to go backwards. However, don't have so much slack that if the colt begins to walk off, you have to gather up three miles of reins before making contact with his mouth.

You may either hold the colt's mane to mount or hold the saddle horn (with a Western saddle). I like to hold the colt's mane because I can feel sooner if he is about to move. Either way is acceptable. Give the colt the command to "stand," and put your left foot in the stirrup. Another cause of mounting problems comes at this step. If you stick your toe straight into the stirrup, it is going to poke the colt in the girth area. This will either make him uncomfortable and he'll try to move to avoid the annoying toe stuck in his girth, or he may interpret it as a signal to go.

Once your hand and foot are in position, it is time to actually spring up into the saddle. Hold the back of the saddle (some people hold the horn with both hands) with your right hand, and fluidly swing your right leg over the colt's rump. Some colts are extremely "goosey" and will bolt if you touch their rump with your right leg as you mount. When your right leg is over the colt, allow your weight and your seat to gently come in contact with the saddle. If the colt stands as you mount, sit quietly and praise him immediately. Then dismount and repeat, praising him when he stands.

If the colt stands three times for you to mount, you'll know that your colt understands the word "stand" and that your training has been effective. You may have to remind him with an occasional lesson, but he is well on the way to becoming a colt that stands still for mounting.

If your colt moves off as you mount, spend additional time teaching him to stand with a saddle and bridle on. If he begins to move off as you are swinging your leg over the saddle, be ready with your rein hand to lift the reins until you feel contact with the colt's mouth to "tell" him to stand. Keep light contact with the reins until you feel the colt halt, then release.

On each succeeding day, you should see an improvement if you have been consistent in showing your colt what is acceptable to you and what is not. The colt may still test you, but you should see at least a slight improvement. Be sure to follow though and continue to train. Insist that the colt stand still for mounting.

After you've settled in the saddle, make him stand for a moment or two, so that he understands to be obedient and to wait for your commands. Then ask the colt to move off at a walk. (You should always walk for a few minutes to warm him up.) Asking a colt to take off at a dead run as soon as you are in the saddle will only teach him to go as soon as you sit. This will add to his prancing and dancing as he waits for you to get into the saddle, defeating the purpose of this stand-for-mounting training.

Another option is to walk him straight into a fence or a wall, or perhaps into a corner. In this case, you must have the ability to use your reins to keep his head straight, pointed at the wall.

Learn patience. Once you have settled in the saddle, relax. Stay alert to your colt's actions and sit quietly on your colt's back for a few minutes. Teach him to relax with you on his back. He must learn that he doesn't have to move every time you get in the saddle, as soon as you get in the saddle.

DISMOUNTING

After you've mounted and enjoyed your ride, it is equally as important for safety reasons for your colt to stand for you to dismount. Tell your colt to whoa to stop him. Once he has stopped all forward motion, tell him to stand. Gather your reins in your left hand with just enough slack so that you are not telling the colt to move backwards, but not so long that you have to gather in a lot of rein to tell him to stop if he takes a step forward. Take your right foot out of the stirrup. If your colt begins to move forward, sit in the saddle and make him back up for three or four steps. Begin again to dismount. If he moves forward, return to the saddle and make him back up again. By making him back up when he wants to go forward, you are telling him that he is wrong. If your colt at some point begins to back up when you dismount, boot him forward for three or four steps. Only when he is standing squarely should you actually dismount. Mount and dismount for as many times as it takes for the colt to stand quietly as you dismount. When he stands quietly, immediately praise him, loosen his girth to make him more comfortable (although not so much that it will slip to one side or the other), and put him away for the day—or untack him and let him graze for ten minutes.

WALK HIM INTO A FENCE

During your initial dismounting training, if the colt won't stand, walk him into a fence. The fence will stop him and you'll have less of a fight on your hands. When he does stand still for dismounting, praise him immediately. As he learns to stand for dismounting, begin to leave two feet between the fence and the colt. Gradually increase the distance between the fence and the colt as he learns to stand still for you to dismount.

REWARD

By rewarding for proper behavior and correcting for bad behavior, you can show a colt what is acceptable. In time, if his lessons are consistent, a colt will find it is easier to obey than to disobey. Training is not always fun or glamorous. Oftentimes it requires a huge amount of patience and persistence to teach even the most basic of good habits. It is easier to teach a young horse the correct way right from the start than to have to go back later and correct bad behavior.

Standing still for mounting and dismounting is a basic procedure but one that often gets overlooked because of its simplicity. Problems sometimes arise because of lack of training or improper training or just plain rider error. Standing still for mounting and dismounting is one way to make your time getting in or out of the saddle safer.

Teaching the proper way to stand for mounting is also one more way of teaching a colt discipline and showing him that he must wait for, and obey, your commands. Training takes a commitment of time, a large dose of patience, and the ability to time your corrections and rewards. Horses don't often intentionally do things to make you angry. Most of the time they are just being horses. They want to get their work over with so that they may return to their stable or pasture and graze or laze about.

CHAPTER ELEVEN

The First Ride

◆

Your colt has spent the last two years playing, growing, and developing and is now ready to ride. Throughout those first two years, you've taught your colt to respect you and your commands. You've longed, saddled, and bridled your colt and then worked on ground driving him. These are all important steps to master before you mount for the first time.

Your colt should freeze when you say the word "whoa" and move forward from a cluck or kiss. He should willingly lead, tie, and be obedient to your commands. He's learned to carry a saddle, a bit, and a bridle without a fuss. He should know to longe and walk, jog, lope, and halt on command. From longeing, you've progressed to longeing with two lines and eventually to ground driving. Here, your colt learned that even when you are behind him, he must obey your cues to move forward and the rein signals to turn left, right, and halt.

Your vet has checked to see if the colt's knees are closed. If his knees are still open, you delay your decision to ride until he is physically ready to carry weight. If his knees were open, he would get sore from the additional weight (and work) and would become resentful. Also, ask your vet to check his teeth for sharp edges or wolf teeth that could interfere with bitting.

Longe your colt before the first ride with a saddle on his back.

RIDING IS JUST ONE MORE DAY

Finally, the day is here. It is time to mount up for the first time. Does your heart flutter at the thought? After following the above sequence, from longeing to ground driving, your horse should be mentally prepared for the first ride. If you think of riding as additional training—just one more day in the training process—*you* will be less apprehensive. *You must stay relaxed to tell your horse to remain relaxed.* Riding is just one more step in the horse's training. If you tense, you tell your horse to be afraid. If you remain relaxed, your horse will remain relaxed.

Your colt's mental attitude should now be such that he respects you and your cues. He has been taught to submit to leading, to longeing, and to carrying the weight of the saddle. The next step is riding. Most babies, when mounted for the first time, do nothing more than stop and possibly sniff your foot to see how your leg got in such an awkward position.

This does not mean that you should not be prepared. There is always an element of danger in working with horses, even the best of them. But riding a colt for the first time, if you've taught him to obey your commands, should progress as easily as the steps taken to get him to this point.

USING A ROUND PEN

I feel that a round pen is the best place to start a colt. It is an enclosed area with no corners for the colt to stop in. After the first few minutes, I can have my assistant remove the lead rope and let me ride the colt alone. On the one occasion when I started a horse (an eight-year-old Arab that had been sat on but had never actually been ridden) without a round pen, I asked my son (a farrier who knows horses and how to ride and train) to ride and I kept a longe line attached to the horse. A knowledgeable ground person is vital, if you choose to ride in the open, especially on an older, unbroken horse.

To do this without a round pen, I would stress that both rider and assistant must be very experienced with horses. Most colts accept riding as part of training, but don't take unnecessary chances. Using a longe line if you do not have a round pen available is a wise move *if* you have a knowledgeable person on the end of the longe line. Otherwise, you are probably better off to take your chances without a longeing assistant.

The time when most colts buck or really act up is when they are saddled for the first time. They must learn to accept the girth around their barrel and that the saddle does not come off when they run, buck, or jump. This is the day to expect fireworks. Be careful at this point. I saddle my colts in the round pen and longe them right there. The worst colt, as far as initially accepting a saddle, flipped over backwards in the round pen so quickly that I had no time to stop him. Yet, when I rode him for the first time, he did nothing. He was easily trained and remembered all that he had been taught.

Some colts will buck the first time that they are ridden and some will not. Be prepared in either case. When you have a helper longe the colt, be sure that he or she keeps control of the longe line so that the colt can't hook a leg over it and get tangled up in it. The longe line becomes more of a danger at that point. Be sure that the colt is given enough line so that the *assistant* is out of the way.

Find your hard hat and use it for this first ride for safety reasons. You never know what reaction you might get. A young colt can fool you. He may seem calm and quiet, only to explode at an inopportune time. It is best to always expect the worst and be prepared.

If you haven't been using a breast collar, add that to your colt's equipment. Most colts have not yet developed withers and adding a breast collar will help to stabilize your saddle. If the colt takes a quick turn, a breast collar will help to keep the saddle where it should be, rather than under the colt's belly— not a good situation.

USE AN ASSISTANT

When you are ready to mount and ride for the first time, you need a knowledgeable person to hold the colt—one who knows horses and has experience in controlling them and one who is able to stay in a safe position instinctively. The assistant must be prepared for anything because colts are unpredictable. The assistant must be able to read the colt and know how to react.

The assistant should have a long cotton lead line or longe line attached to the colt's halter. As mentioned previously, I prefer cotton to nylon because it is not as likely to burn your hand. The assistant holds one hand on the line close to the halter (but never on the snap where it could inadvertently be unsnapped). The balance of the line should be coiled in large loops in the other hand so that it is not dragging where the assistant may trip on it. *Never* wrap a rope tightly around your hand, in any situation, or you could get dragged.

STAND UP IN THE STIRRUP

Ask your helper to make a fist, push it into the colt's neck, and hold his or her arm stiffly. This will allow the assistant to stay away from the colt if he spooks. Stand up in the stirrup, rub the colt's neck, and pat his off side. When he feels relaxed, swing your leg well over his rump (being careful not to touch his rump because some colts are quite goosey). Sit gently in the saddle. Don't spook the colt at this point by unnecessary force. Carefully and gently find your other stirrup. When riding a baby for the first time, put weight into your heels, brace your legs a little forward, and lean slightly backward. This is a safer position to be in and may keep you from going over his head on the slight chance he decides to explode.

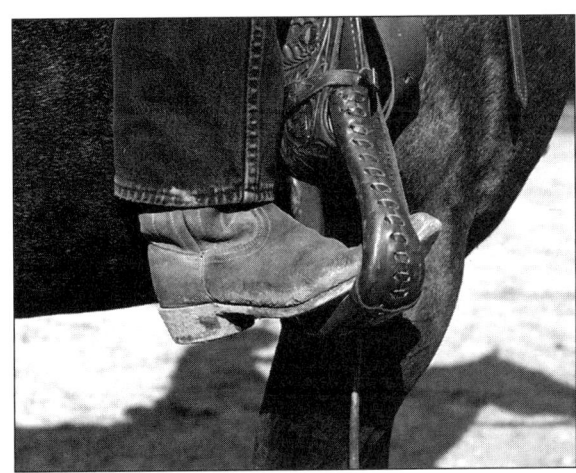

Keep your weight a little braced back and your heels down.

When you are in the saddle, wiggle your weight back and forth just a little to let the colt know that, "Yes, there is now a person on your back." Talk to the colt in a soothing voice. This way he won't forget that you are on his back. Scratch his neck without letting go of the reins, and be careful not to pull on his mouth. I don't ask a colt to stand still for too long on the first ride. Ask your assistant to use the lead line to move the colt forward sharply to the right, keeping his hand or fist pushed into the colt's neck. This sharp bend in the colt's body can keep him from bucking. Walk two or three steps, say "whoa" and halt. Scratch the colt on his neck and tell him that he is good boy. Repeat the same forward steps again to the right. Again, halt and reward. Continue walking for three to six steps and halting for two to three small circles to the right. Then reverse the process and circle to the left, using the same sequence of cues.

PAY ATTENTION

The ground person must be prepared for anything and must be able to snap the colt back if he rushes or be able to keep his head up if necessary. Your helper cannot be afraid or the colt will be able to tell through the assistant's tone of voice. Your ground person must demand respect yet act as if this is just one more step in the colt's training.

RELAX

You as the rider must be relaxed to tell the colt that all is okay. If your body tenses, your body language tells the colt to be afraid. This is extremely important. You can turn what should be a quick and easy ride into a nightmare. If you are tense or afraid, find a knowledgeable person and ask him or her to ride this first time. Most of these first rides go smoothly. But there is always a chance of the colt exploding. A knowledgeable rider should be able to ride it out and let the colt know that bucking is unacceptable. If the colt bolts in a round pen, sit relaxed and ride it out. This is an important step in the colt's training and must be treated as such.

As long as the colt accepts being walked in tight circles when he is mounted, begin to enlarge the circles. Have your

Sit relaxed to tell your colt to relax.

assistant longe the colt in small circles. Then take control and use your legs combined with a cluck to ask for forward motion and use your reins lightly to signal a halt. If the colt accepts this (you can tell by the feel of him and by the position of his head and ears), ask your assistant to longe the colt, but only if you've decided that you feel more confident longeing the colt before removing the longe line on this first ride. I find it just as easy to unsnap the line and ride alone from this point. In this way, I only have myself to worry about and I can ride the colt without having to give instructions to my helper.

Once the colt is out in the longeing circle, use *your* rein and leg cues to ask the colt to walk, trot, and canter. Your helper can add your normal longeing cues (a cluck, kiss, or whip cues) if the colt doesn't respond, but eventually, you want to control the colt with your own cues from his back. Depending on your level of comfort, you can unsnap the longe line or continue to longe the colt for another day or two.

Once you feel comfortable with the colt's response, ask your assistant to remove the longe line. Ride the colt around the pen, teaching him to turn and to stop. If he won't stop, turn him into the fence and let the fence actually stop him. Hold a rein in each hand and "hold his head between your hands," keeping his nose pointed at the fence. (If he tries to turn left, correct with a direct right rein and vice versa.) This way you do not have to pull on his mouth to stop, a signal that he has only *started* to understand from ground driving.

When you ask a colt to turn, pull out with the rein, not back. But do make the colt turn. He must understand that he *must* turn from the rein signal. If he only bends his head and neck, pull his head around until you get two or three steps of turning. Quickly release the pressure to reward him, then ask again. Releasing pressure as soon as he responds shows him that he performed as required and that he will get rewarded for turning. You can refine this exaggerated aid later when he understands.

WALK, JOG, AND LOPE

I ask a colt to walk, jog, and lope on the first day. He must learn to do all three. You create more problems by going too slowly and waiting for weeks or months before you ask for a lope. However, your comfort level determines how quickly you should proceed. If you are nervous, your colt will be nervous. Don't push for more than you are comfortable with. And if for any reason your colt will not guide or halt at the jog or trot, don't expect him to guide at the lope or canter. This is another reason why a round pen or small arena is helpful when starting a colt. The fence more or less guides the colt initially so that you can ask for at least a few canter or lope strides. But again, fix your guiding problems at the slower gaits if you are in a wide-open space. Spend a few days working out any problems at the slower gaits before you proceed. But remember that a lope is much easier to sit to than a fast trot. And do not post to the trot on a green colt because it is an unsafe position. If you are out of the saddle and the colt bucks or spooks, you may go off.

If the colt is extremely spooky or nervous, or if he feels really out of balance, I may only walk and jog and save the lope for the next day. But I don't wait too long to lope. However, you should adapt this program to suit your comfort level. The colt needs to learn to lope. If you are afraid, find a knowledgeable person to ride the colt.

If the colt bolts, sit relaxed and ride it out. This is why I start in the round pen. The fence will make him go around and there should be no rocks or obstacles in your way. By sitting relaxed, you tell the colt that everything is all right. Given time, he will slow down and relax and you may teach a potentially hot and anxious equine to understand from the beginning that there is nothing to be afraid of and to relax.

You must be a good rider and have good balance. You should be able to ride without needing to squeeze your legs to hang on. You don't want to scare the colt. This first ride sets the tone for the horse's future training and is important.

Turn your colt into the fence if he won't stop.

The colt must learn to be obedient under saddle. I work a colt harder on this first day than I do on the following days because I want him to learn to stop and go, to turn left and right, and to walk, jog/trot, or canter/lope. When I feel he that understands slightly, I dismount and let him think about it overnight. I never rush a colt to learn new behavior, because he has a short attention span, and can only digest so much on a given day. But I do like to teach briefly those lessons on the first day. On the following days, I back off somewhat and let the colt tell me where he needs work.

LACK OF FORWARD MOVEMENT

If a colt does not move forward, use your legs and *bump* his sides continuously in a rhythm—bump, bump, bump, bump—until he moves forward. *As soon as* he moves forward, stop bumping and sit quietly. Timing is important! As soon as the colt begins to go forward at your chosen gait, you must immediately reward him by ceasing your cues. This is the only way that he can understand that he responded properly. The colt will learn that if he moves, the bumping stops and he is rewarded. You may need to use a crop to tap his rump so that he understands he must move forward. You must make him move forward! Teach him what is acceptable behavior. Bad behavior today will be harder to fix tomorrow. A horse that does not go forward is not a pleasure to ride. Teach him right from the start that he must obey!

These first lessons are brief—ten to fifteen minutes at a time. I ask the colt to turn left, right, and to halt a few times. Then I ask him to walk, jog, and lope in each direction. Once that is accomplished, I dismount to reward him, showing him that riding is not a big deal and that he will get rewarded for behaving in an acceptable manner.

IF HE BOLTS

A lesson may be longer on a horse that bolts. You will need to sit on his back and wait for him to slow down. If you jerk on the reins to stop him, he will associate riding with being hurt and therefore be afraid. Your next ride will be that much tougher because he has had a bad experience. Do your best to make this first ride pleasant.

REWARD THE COLT

When the colt has done what you asked of him, stop him, sit on his back for a moment, pat his neck, then dismount to reward him. Be careful when you dismount. Some horses will go through the entire ride quietly and then will panic when you dismount. Be prepared for anything. After dismounting,

Reward your colt with a loose rein for responding well.

mount again. Sit on his back, pat his neck, dismount and put him away. When I untack a colt, I give him a good brushing to let him know that I am pleased.

PLAN FOR A FUTURE RIDE

Depending on what happens on this first ride, I plan my next lesson with this colt. Some colts may need work on turning, while others may need work on moving forward. Read what your colt tells you and plan accordingly. Remember to sit relaxed to tell the colt not to be afraid. This is one of the most important lessons of his life, and will start him on the right path.

Only use your cues or aids to tell the colt to change what he is doing. For example, if the colt is walking correctly, sit quietly and enjoy the ride. When you want him to jog, only then should you apply the aids to tell him to jog. As soon as he starts to jog, release your aids and let him jog. Only when you want him to turn should you pick up rein contact and ask him to turn. As soon as he turns, release all rein pressure and sit quietly. In this way, you are teaching him to be light, obedient, and responsive.

On each progressive day, refine your aids. As the horse gains understanding, add new training procedures to his lessons. Keep him learning so that he doesn't become bored. Teach your horse to turn left from a left direct rein, but apply the right neck rein cue as well (on a horse that you wish to teach to neck rein). In this way, he will learn both cues. Use your legs as you would on an older horse so that he begins to associate leg cues with the proper response. Use the same cues as you would on an older horse and save training time.

Starting a colt this way will give him a chance to become a pleasant member of the equine family. If you run into problems along the way, my best advice is to get help immediately from a knowledgeable trainer. It is easier to fix a colt that has not developed repeated bad habits. Money spent now for a month's training will pay off down the road. The colt's initiation to life under saddle is the starting point of his future training and should be treated accordingly.

CHAPTER TWELVE

The First Thirty Days

———————— ◆ ————————

A colt's general attitude toward riding should be that it is just another day of training and nothing to get excited about. A colt must learn to obey your cues, whether you are on the ground or on his back. During the first thirty days under saddle, you will do nothing more than teach a colt the basic cues and that riding is a pleasant experience. After the initial rides under saddle, you begin to teach various cues that a well-trained horse must understand, but these cues are exaggerated—not the light and barely seen cues used on a finished horse. At this stage of the game, you only want the colt to understand that he must respect your cues and obey them, whether you are on the ground or on his back. When the colt understands the basics—going forward, turning left and right, and halting—then you begin to ask the colt to progress to more advanced training. (You may omit using the additional neck-rein cue if you have no desire for your horse to learn this aid.)

By asking a colt to walk, jog, lope, halt, and turn both left and right on the first day, he will learn that these actions will be expected of him. Be sure to ask a colt to jog and lope periodically. Don't work only at a walk. The colt will then think that he must only walk under saddle. Jogging or loping around the rail and across the pen from time to time will teach him that he must do all three. A colt must learn that jogging and loping are part of being ridden and nothing to get excited about.

RESPECT

Training demands a colt's respect, but respect does not mean fear. A colt should trust you and know that you will not harm him. However, you must demand that he behaves in a way that is acceptable to you. Acceptable equine behavior does not include bolting, ignoring your aids, nipping, kicking or treating you as his playmate. He must learn to respect and obey your requests immediately upon your asking. Rewarding him, whether through release of all aids or a brief period of rest, will reinforce in his mind that he performed to your satisfaction.

You must be prepared to get your point across. Use the least amount of pressure first, then increase the amount of pressure until a colt responds correctly. Knowing how and when to apply this rule is crucial, and for this reason, having a good idea of what is and what is not acceptable equine behavior is beneficial both to you and to the colt. Don't be afraid to ask questions of people who are more knowledgeable than you. Study as many good horse-and-rider teams as you can and watch the way in which they interact with each other.

Early training lays the basis for the balance of a colt's life. If a colt performs a maneuver three or four times, it is a habit, whether it is good or bad. It is easier to teach good habits from the beginning rather than to break a bad habit later. During the first thirty days, you'll begin to teach a colt various aids. For safety reasons, this early training should be done in a round pen or other small enclosed area. Only when he responds readily to your command to halt and will turn both to the left and to the right should you begin to take him to larger areas. Moving out of a small, enclosed area will further his education and keep him from learning to depend on a fence. Also, if he is kept in a round pen for too long, he will learn to drop his shoulder and fall into his circles. He must learn to walk, jog, or lope in straight lines. By the end of thirty days, depending on the colt, he should be ready to move to a bigger arena. Remember that your safety comes first. Be sure that your colt responds well to the whoa command.

ENFORCE YOUR AIDS

Exaggerate your aids when you first begin to ride a colt. If you want him to turn, bring your direct rein out (not up or back), gain contact, pull his head in the correct direction by guiding him with the direct rein, then release. Continue to guide and release. Make the colt think. Don't do his work for him by pulling him around an entire circle. To turn him to the left, direct rein holding your left rein about six to ten inches (out to the side) away from the saddle. In addition, on a Western horse (so that he also begins to associate the neck-rein cue with turning), place the neck rein across his neck as you turn. Be sure that you do not pull so hard on the neck rein that it turns his head in the opposite direction in which you wish to go. As the colt is turning in a circle to the left, bend him around your inside leg. Use just enough pressure on your inside leg so that he feels it and therefore begins to learn that legs mean more than just "Go."

Bring your rein out initially and exaggerate your aids to show the colt what you want.

Every time you ride, use your aids consistently because horses learn by repetition. Be fair to your colt. Use your hand and leg aids the same way, every time. Your colt will soon learn that a left direct rein signal means to turn left—if you reward him by releasing pressure when he responds to the rein cue to turn left. As you feel the colt becoming lighter and more responsive to your aids, begin to use lighter pressure. This rewards him for doing as you ask and tells him that he is correct.

By using the same aids on a colt as you would on an older horse, you'll save training time. For example, if you never lay the neck-rein cue on his neck until long after he responds to a direct pull, you will then have to spend additional time teaching him this new neck-rein cue. If you use the neck-rein cue from the beginning, he will begin to associate it with turning. If you never put a leg on a colt except to tell him to go faster, he will then have to relearn that legs can mean more than just "Go."

If you follow the suggestions in this book and teach your colt to jog from the cluck and lope from the kiss while on the longe line, he should readily respond to those same cues when he is mounted. (You can use your own set of cues as long as you use them consistently.) You will help your colt to understand leg cues by using the cluck for a jog, as well as the "new" mounted leg cue (which means to jog), and the kiss for a lope

Let him jog on a loose rein; sit relaxed to tell him that all is well.

along with the leg cue to lope. For a jog, I use both legs, squeezing my calves and only using both heels to bump if he doesn't respond. I use my outside heel to ask for a lope on the inside lead. (Right heel for left lead, and vice versa.) This system helps the colt to learn new cues by associating an "old" cue (the cluck or kiss) with a new cue (legs).

Later, you can refine these aids. For a colt's first rides under saddle, help him by relying on previously taught cues. Ask a colt to jog by first squeezing both legs, immediately followed by a clucking sound. Continue to repeat this lesson so that the colt learns to associate both cues with jogging. If he doesn't jog from the cluck, bump your legs on his sides to make it uncomfortable for him not to jog. As soon as he starts to jog, immediately stop bumping. Sit quietly on his back to reward him for jogging and let him jog around the arena a few times. He'll soon learn that the bumping stops when he jogs. The same principle is true for the lope. Ask him to lope by first using your normal outside leg cue, followed by a kissing sound. If he doesn't respond and lope, bump him forward with both legs into a lope. When he does lope, sit quietly to tell him that he responded correctly. Eventually, he will learn to lope on a light signal from your outside leg to avoid getting bumped by your legs.

I ask a colt to walk, jog, and lope on the first day. You can see by my rein position that he has freedom of his head, but I can pick up contact easily if I get into trouble.

WHOA

If a colt will not halt when you say "Whoa!" keep his head lightly between your reins, or hold a rein in either hand and direct him into the fence, letting the fence actually stop him. You need to hold your hands about six to eight inches from either side of the saddle horn so that you can guide his head into the fence. Remember that this is training, not equitation. Your hands and/or legs may not always be in the correct equitation position. You must exaggerate your aids in the beginning to show the colt what you want. Later, you can refine those aids to acceptable equitation.

Here I've turned my colt and exaggerated my rein cue, showing you how to stop if the verbal/rein signal isn't effective.

Some of the rules of equitation do apply, however. By sitting deeply in the saddle with your weight balanced over your heels, your body is in a position to react to whatever moves a colt might make. The first three or four days, I ride a little behind the motion of the colt (my legs slightly forward and my weight slightly back). If a colts start to buck, I can brace my legs forward and ride it out. When I begin to trust that the colt will not react badly, I ride in a more balanced manner. Remember not to tense your body as if you are nervous. Your colt will feel it and it will make him nervous. Stay quiet and relaxed so that the colt will stay quiet and relaxed.

STAY BALANCED

A colt has to learn how to carry your weight and how to balance with you in the saddle. It can take weeks or months for him to become comfortable with your weight in the saddle. At first he will wobble from side to side when you ask him to go in a straight line, not only from carrying your weight but also because he must be taught to travel in a straight line. This is perfectly normal. In time, he will learn to balance your weight and do all of the things that you take for granted with an older horse.

If you cannot ride balanced in the saddle, take additional lessons before you start a colt. To understand the reasoning for this, pick up a jump pole. If you lift it in the center, it balances and is easy to carry. However, if you have more weight at one end or the other, one end is going to drag on the ground and put you off balance. You can also have someone sit on your back and lean from side to side as you walk forward—it will give you a greater understanding of your colt's experience.

REVIEW YOUR PAST LESSONS

Before mounting your colt on each following lesson, think of what he "told" you on the previous ride. Did he move too fast? If so, plan a day of slow work, longeing him prior to work if necessary. Walk in large circles to teach him to obey your cues. Then ask him to halt. Stand for a moment to reward him for halting. This will also let him realize that there is nothing to fear. Continue going slow and easy, walking, bending, and halting. Reward him for good behavior. When he seems to respond readily to your cue to halt, ask him to jog a large circle, then have him halt. Reward him immediately. Always halt in a different place so that the colt doesn't anticipate stopping in a certain spot. Teach him that a halt means a rest for him.

If a colt was too quiet and didn't understand or tried to ignore your cues to go forward, ask him to jog in straight lines or circles—or any configuration—to teach him he must go forward on your command. Bump his sides with your legs *and continue to bump* to make him uncomfortable—until he jogs. As soon as he starts to jog, stop bumping to let him learn that he is rewarded when he jogs. Then ask him to lope using the same sequence of cues. If he doesn't respond to your cues, use a crop to tap on his rump. Don't use the ends of your reins or you could inadvertently pull on his mouth.

When the colt learns to be guided by your reins, make circles, figure-eights, and serpentines. Riding around the outside edge of the arena only teaches a colt to depend on a fence. He must learn to listen to and obey your cues.

Ask a colt to walk, jog, and lope in large circles. If you ask your colt to lope and he departs on the wrong lead, allow him to lope for a minute, then gently bring him back to a walk. Ask him to lope again, bending his nose into the circle. If he again takes the incorrect lead, let him lope a half circle and then gently bring him back to a walk. This time, lift his outside shoulder by lifting up your outside rein. Do not tip his nose to the outside; lift his shoulder up by lifting up the rein. In the beginning, ask for a lope on a corner if you are not in a round pen.

If he will not take one lead, look first for a physical problem. Is his "leading" leg—or hoof—sore? Is his strike-off leg sore? A canter or lope is a three-beat gait. When taking a left lead, the horse initiates the lope by striking off with his right hind leg. This is followed by the second beat, the diagonal pair of left hind leg and right foreleg, followed by his leading left foreleg. Ask the colt to lope on the longe line. See if he will take that lead while unmounted. If he does this easily, then it very well could be a riding or training problem. Be sure that you are sitting balanced and centered. If the colt will not take the lead while longeing, look further for a physical problem. Barring that, work the colt on his bad or stiff side to help him learn to use it.

Never punish or scare a colt for taking a wrong lead. First he must learn to lope, and then *later, you may teach him to lope on a correct lead.* If you pull him back to a walk as soon as he takes a wrong lead, he might think that he is being punished for loping. How is he to understand in these first days that he must not only lope but lope on a particular lead as well? I let the colt lope so that he understands and is rewarded for loping. Later, I work on fixing the lead problem.

THINK

Spend a lot of time thinking about what you are telling your colt through your actions. While a colt must respect your cues, do not frighten him or punish him for something that he can't yet understand. Think! Each and every time you ride, think of what you want to accomplish. If on the previous day your colt refused to turn to the right, spend time turning to the right. When the colt behaves and turns to the right on your command, stop and sit quietly on his back for a moment to reward him. Then go on to something else. Later, you may come back and see if the colt understands what it is that you were trying to fix. Don't drill, drill, drill on a maneuver. Horses learn by repetition, but not by being drilled incessantly.

If you have planned something for your lesson, yet your colt seems to have a problem with an earlier step, *change your plans and work on that.* It may take five minutes to correct a step, or it may take three days. Let the colt tell you at what speed to proceed. Your initial plan may need to wait. Have a plan of what you want to accomplish over a period of time, but let the colt tell you when he is ready to proceed. After he understands a new maneuver or lesson, add a slight degree of difficulty from time to time to keep his mind fresh. Don't confuse a colt by drilling something into his head over and over again once he has performed to the best of his ability. This could make him think that he has performed incorrectly and is being punished. Keep him interested and wanting to learn. Your lessons should be geared with the colt in mind.

Reward for good behavior. Although you might have to exaggerate in the beginning, do begin to lighten up your aids as a colt shows that he understands.

Try to consistently end your lesson on a good note. Never let a colt get away with something and then put him away because this is rewarding him for his misbehavior. I find it helpful to teach a colt new aids or cues near the end of his lesson. When he seems to begin to grasp the new concept, dismount and put him away. This leaves it fresh in his mind and allows him time to think. Most young horses will perform the new maneuver quite readily the next day.

IMPORTANT POINTS

The important points to remember when starting a colt are:

- Consistency: Use the same aids, the same way, every time.
- *"Ask"* a colt to perform first: Use a light signal or aid.
- If he doesn't respond to that light aid or cue,*"tell"* him to perform using a somewhat stronger aid.
- If he still hasn't obeyed your request, *enforce* your command. This may mean a whack from a crop or a bat on his rump, holding your rein hand on your hip until he does turn, or in some way showing the colt that it is in his best interest to obey. Although he must learn to obey, give him the opportunity to respond to a light cue first.
- Reward. When he does perform correctly or to the best of his ability be sure to reward him to tell him that he performed correctly. In this way, he will respond to a light aid to avoid a harsher aid and also to get the reward of release of pressure or a brief rest.

LET THE COLT ENJOY THE FIRST RIDES

The first thirty days should be an enjoyable experience for a colt. Don't scare him or sour him for life with this new experience of being ridden. The initial lessons are spent:

- Showing the colt that he must obey your commands when mounted as well as from the ground.
- Learning these new aids given from his back.
- Learning to balance and carry your weight.

Neck-Rein Training

◆

I f your colt is headed for a career as a reiner, Western pleasure or Western riding horse, or even as a trail horse (either English or Western), you will want to teach him to neck rein. Your colt must learn to obey this signal—one that is slightly more difficult to understand, at least initially. Direct reining "forces" or "pulls" the colt's nose in the direction in which you choose to go and his body *should* follow. Neck reining is a programmed response—a signal to obey a particular cue.

When I begin to ride a colt that I want to neck rein, I begin to neck rein on the very first day. This initiates the colt to the neck-rein signal and therefore is not something that I have to start to introduce at a later date. It thus saves some time.

START NEAR A FENCE

To actually teach a colt to neck rein, I start in the round pen. Any enclosed area, free of rocks or obstacles, with a fence that you can get close to will suffice. A long, straight section of fence will also work, if that is what is available.

RIDE IN A SNAFFLE

Neck-rein training starts in a snaffle. A snaffle bit—a bit with no shanks—works off of the corners of a colt's mouth.

This allows you to "pull" the colt around as you ask him to turn. Additionally, as you "pull" the colt around, you also use the neck-rein cue to begin to teach him to obey it as he turns.

LET HIM SETTLE FIRST

First longe or ride your colt so that he is settled and willing to work. To actually teach the neck-rein signal, walk your colt in a straight line along the fence—about three feet to the inside of the fence. For this first example, we will walk with the fence on our right. Separate your reins, putting one rein in each hand. With your right hand—the one closest to the fence—direct rein or "pull" the horse into the fence, forcing him to turn back into the fence and walk back in the opposite direction. At the same time, place your left rein, or neck-rein cue, over his neck. I use my inside leg—in this case, my right leg—to bend the colt around. Use light pressure with your leg at the girth to "break the colt in the middle" as he bends around your leg going around the turn. Your outside leg should do nothing at this point unless the colt begins to lag and slow down. Then bump him with your outside heel behind the girth to create forward momentum, forcing him to continue walking to make the turn and head back in the other direction. You might also use your outside leg if the colt is

Turn the colt into the fence with a direct rein, but apply the neck-rein cue as well.

At this point, or slightly before, release your direct cue and let the fence turn the colt.

throwing his hip to the outside of your circle. In this case, his hindquarters would swing out to the left rather than follow the bend or arch of the circle to the right. Use a strong "holding" outside leg behind the girth. This will hold the colt's hindquarters in place and make his back end follow his front end around the corner.

When the colt is committed to the turn—when his head is slightly past right angles to the fence—release your right, inside, direct-rein pressure. The fence will actually force the colt to turn. Don't rely on the direct-rein "pull" to make him turn. Be sure to keep your neck rein in place throughout the entire turn. Once the colt completely makes the turn and is walking straight down the fence (he should now be walking with the fence on your left), release all cues. This shows him that the neck-rein cue means to turn. When he completes the turn and is walking straight, and all cues and pressure are released, he feels rewarded for obeying the cue and making the turn.

RELEASE THE CUE

Be sure that as soon as your colt makes the turn and begins to walk straight in the opposite direction, you release your neck-rein cue and all leg cues so that the colt understands that the neck-rein cue is only meant to tell him to turn. Keep your body relaxed to tell the colt he responded correctly.

If a colt tries to scoot out from under you because you used too much leg pressure, repeat the maneuver being sure to use less pressure. Each colt responds differently to different amounts of leg pressure. You will have to find what works best on your colt. Some need barely a whisper of pressure and some will need a good bump. Experiment to find what your colt responds to best.

SIT RELAXED

Sit relaxed to tell the colt that this new maneuver is nothing to be afraid of and to tell him to relax. If your body is tense, your colt will feel it and he will be tense. If he is too quiet and tries to stop when you send him down the fence in a straight line, use both legs to send him forward. Think of squeezing his energy out the front.

After the colt walks about twenty feet down the fence and is settled and paying attention, repeat the entire sequence of cues, using the opposite aids to turn the colt in the opposite direction. If it takes more time for your colt to settle initially as he learns this new maneuver, let him walk forward for as many feet as it takes for him to settle. It is the actual turning into the fence that trains him, not the distance in between asking him to change directions. Stop and sit on the colt's back to relax him if he becomes "hot" or excited, or walk in small circles to relax his mind. Take your time. Let the colt absorb this new request at his own pace. After a few times, he'll understand that it is not a big deal and nothing to get excited about.

TRAINING REQUIRES PATIENCE

Training a colt requires patience and the repetition of cues. If you lose your temper or your patience, your body will tense, and you will tell the colt to be afraid. You will never be able to train effectively if you are tense or angry. You send conflicting signals to a colt that way. Horses read our body language much more than we think and oftentimes much more than we are aware of.

Once you've mastered the sequence of direct rein, neck rein, and inside leg, and have mastered the timing of the release of the direct-rein signal, continue to turn right into the fence, walk down the fence, then turn left into the fence, for ten or fifteen times. When the colt shows signs of understanding and is acting quietly, stop him and sit on his back for a minute or two. Sit relaxed, though not so relaxed that you have no control if he spooks or runs off. Your safety is always your first concern.

Sit with your body relaxed to tell the colt that he responded correctly and can now enjoy a well-deserved rest. He'll appreciate the reward and will try to please you in the future to gain the reward of a rest and the release of pressure.

NEVER STOP WHEN A COLT IS PERFORMING BADLY

On the same note, never stop when the colt is fighting you or tossing his head or acting in an unacceptable manner. Always try to stop the colt after he responded or tried to respond to the best of his ability. Reward him for good behavior, not for bad behavior.

After rewarding the colt, go on to something else for five or ten minutes, although you should place the neck rein over the colt's neck whenever you turn. Then come back to the fence and repeat the entire series of cues. Direct rein with one hand until the colt is committed to the turn and remember to release as soon as possible once his head is in such a position that he must turn. Keep him close enough to the fence so that when his head is turned in the direction that you wish to go, he has to turn. Either leave him no choice, or make his choice easy by staying close to the fence. This closeness to the fence helps by showing him that it is the only way to turn comfortably.

Use your neck rein with enough pressure so that the colt can feel it, but don't use so much pressure that you pull the bit in the opposite direction of that in which you wish to go.

After two to three weeks of practicing this maneuver four to five times a week at a walk, you should see signs that your colt is beginning to understand the neck-rein signal. When you feel the colt responding and turning, use your direct rein less and less. Give your colt a brief hesitation (on your part) to obey the neck-rein signal before you "remind" him with the direct-rein signal.

GO ON TO THE JOG

Once he understands at a walk, begin to ask the colt to jog and to obey the neck-rein signal at a jog. You will have to increase your distance from the fence so that the colt can jog and turn in toward the fence as he changes directions. The distance from the fence will vary from colt to colt—his speed, athletic ability, and length of stride will influence how far away you must be.

Any time you increase your speed, you are increasing the degree of difficulty. Your colt may not yet respond at these faster gaits. Continue to ride with two hands on the reins so that you may add a direct-rein signal if the colt doesn't respond to the neck-rein signal. Use your legs in the same manner, bending around your inside leg on the tighter turns and lightening up your leg pressure on the larger turns. Use your outside leg to bump him around the turns if he slows or hesitates, but remember to vary the amount of leg pressure you need until you find what works best on your colt.

Remind your colt to obey the neck rein by picking up light contact with the direct rein, and only then "pulling" him in the

After he understands turning off the fence, help him to understand this new cue in the center of the pen.

Until eventually you can go to a shank bit and turn the colt one-handed.

direction that you wish to go, *if* he ignores the neck-rein signal. Always gain contact first, then guide gently him. You can "pull" the rein as hard as necessary, if you first gain contact with his mouth. Only when he has turned and obeyed your signal to turn should you release the direct-rein pressure. Then go to another turn and ask again, correcting if necessary.

After the colt shows his understanding of the neck-rein signal at the jog near a fence, begin to jog large circles in your arena. Each time that the colt's nose veers from the direction given by the neck-rein signal, pick up light contact and bend his nose in the correct direction. Then release the direct rein. Allow the colt to make a mistake so that you may correct him. Do not do his work for him by pulling him around the entire circle. Make him think and obey the neck-rein signal.

In the beginning, it will seem as if you are almost always direct reining him. The colt is still learning, even though it feels that you are always direct reining him. Continue to pick up contact, bend, and release. Pick up contact, bend, and release. Always keep the appropriate neck-rein cue in place. Over a period of time, you will find that you are correcting or using your direct rein less and less often, and the colt is obeying the neck-rein cue more and more.

The next step is to begin to make large circles, first to the left and then to the right. As you come across the center to change direction, give your colt time to respond to the neck-rein cue before you correct him. As you begin to change direction, give the neck-rein cue and hesitate—wait to see if the colt responds. Then correct him if necessary. This way, the colt has time to absorb the request and react to it. Give him time to understand that if he does not obey the neck-rein signal, he will get corrected by the direct rein. Let him learn that he can avoid the correction by obeying the original light neck-rein cue.

NECK REINING AT THE LOPE

Eventually, you may ask the colt to neck rein at the lope, first loping in circles. The same rules apply. Give your colt plenty of room. Guide him around your corners with a direct rein if necessary and be sure to place the neck rein over his neck. It will take him a bit longer to obey the cue at the lope, so be sure to allow him time to respond before correcting him.

TRAINING TAKES TIME

Teaching a colt to neck rein takes time. It takes time for a colt to learn to respond instantly to a neck-rein signal, or to perform the high-speed turnarounds seen on today's reiners. You will see a small improvement each time you ride, and eventually, the colt will need hardly any reminders at all. Take your time, have patience, and show the colt the correct response by rewarding him appropriately.

Remember to pick up contact lightly, then correct. Jerking on a colt's mouth serves no purpose in training. It hurts the horse, makes him fearful of the bit, and can permanently damage a colt's mouth. It can make him angry or resentful of training. If a colt is angry or hurting, his mind will be on the pain and not on what you are trying to teach him. "Talk" to your colt softly. By going slowly and letting the fence actually turn the colt in the initial stages of neck-rein training, your colt will learn this new cue or signal and will turn easily with one hand on the reins.

CHAPTER FOURTEEN

Transitions

———— ◆ ————

Transitions—changing from one gait to another such as from a walk to a jog to a lope—or from a walk to a trot to a canter—will keep your colt paying attention and learning. Riding off the rail in circles and serpentines, and simply zigzagging the ring, will also keep your colt obedient, alert, and waiting for your next command.

If, after initially breaking your colt, you ride in an arena and jog or trot around and around and around the rail, your colt is only learning to balance your weight and to depend on the fence as a guideline. He should be listening and waiting for your cues—not only the cue to tell him *where* to go next, but *at what speed.* Riding the rail will build condition, but it will not build mental ability or increase a colt's level of training that much. We call riding the rail "joy riding." There is a limited amount of work done by both horse and rider, and both can get bored rather quickly.

During a colt's early days under saddle, he *should* be allowed to stay in a gait for a longer period of time so that he learns *what* is expected of him. In the early stages under saddle, he needs that time to learn to balance your weight and to learn the proper response to these new mounted cues. Changing too

Taking your colt and riding in the wide open spaces teaches him not to depend on a fence.

often in the beginning stages will only confuse him. Yet, once a colt does understand the cues for each gait and is comfortable performing at each gait, he should be asked to change or to make transitions so that he learns to pay attention and doesn't become bored with his work. Slowly increase the frequency of your requests. If the colt show signs of being resentful or confused, back up a step and wait a week or two.

WORKING WITH THE QUIET COLT

A quiet colt, the type that tends to get lazy and bored quickly, will benefit if early in his training you begin to ask him to change from one gait to another and to change direction. This will keep him interested and learning. A "hotter" type of colt will benefit more from slower, consistent work with long stretches of staying at the same gait so that he can settle.

Ask the quieter type of colt to obey your cues as quickly as he can at that point in time, teaching him to be alert for the smallest command. Loping or cantering from time to time will also help to keep a quiet colt from falling asleep or becoming bored.

WORKING WITH A "HOTTER" COLT

If your colt is "hot" or easily excited, riding in the same gait for an extended period of time will help to teach him to settle down. He'll learn that there is no reason to get excited—no surprises, such as being asked to change to a new gait, are coming until he is comfortable with what he is doing. Later, once he is more solid under saddle, introduce the maneuvers that you do sooner on a quieter colt.

RIDING THE FIRST THIRTY DAYS

I use the first thirty to sixty days teaching a colt that being ridden is nothing more than one more step in his everyday training. I do nothing to hurt him, physically or mentally. I do nothing to push a colt past what he is easily able to give at that point in time. I want him to think that being ridden is enjoyable—that it is nothing to fear and nothing to get upset over.

Forcing a colt to learn maneuvers that are past his physical or mental level too soon in the training process can cause him to become sour or resentful. This can sour him on under saddle work for the rest of his life. Make riding an enjoyable experience for your colt, and he'll enjoy learning new maneuvers or procedures.

Performing jog or lope transitions will keep your colt paying attention. Here, I've exaggerated my outside heel cue— the lope cue.

When your colt has shown you that he is comfortable with his level of training, and has learned to balance your weight and to turn left and right and to halt on command, it is time to make him expect new commands from time to time. He must learn to obey them without question. Begin to introduce increasingly different and difficult maneuvers. Ask the colt to perform transitions from one gait to another and to change directions.

When you reward a colt for a proper response, he learns that it is to his benefit to obey your request for a change of gait or direction. By rewarding a colt promptly (by the release of leg or rein pressure), the colt learns to respond to lighter and lighter cues to gain the relief of pressure sooner. Timing and feel—both of these were discussed in detail in a previous chapter. I combine transitions and changes of direction with teaching a colt to neck rein, to move his hip or to move away from leg pressure, and to be obedient.

WARM HIM UP FIRST

First walk on a loose rein to warm up a colt before you begin your training session. Slowly increase speed and implement bending exercises. This will prepare the colt physically to work as well as help his mental attitude. If a colt thinks that every time he walks into the arena, he will be forced to put in an all-out effort, he'll become scared, sour, or resentful.

I begin by asking a colt to walk around the arena four or five feet away from the fence. I ask him to change directions, turning into the fence. Lift your inside rein to lift the colt's inside shoulder as you turn into the fence. This prevents the colt from falling over his inside shoulder as he turns. For example, circling to the left with the fence on my right, I stay four feet to the inside of the fence and ask the colt to walk. I then lift my right rein to lift the colt's right shoulder and also to direct rein the colt into the fence to change direction. Once I feel the colt's right shoulder lift back and out of the way, giving him room to cross over with his left front leg and make the turn, and I see that his nose is committed to the turn, I release my right rein and let the fence actually force the colt to change directions.

When he understands the cue to lift his shoulder and make the turn at a walk, I increase the degree of difficulty and jog down the fence, halt, walk, and then change directions. I'll "change his mind" from time to time by asking for a complete halt, or perhaps a halt and a backup. Other times, I'll ask him to turn to the inside of the arena. I'll turn both left and right, being sure to spend additional time on the colt's weaker side.

TEACH HIM TO WAIT FOR YOUR COMMAND

The colt begins to pay attention when I ask for a change because he is unsure if I will ask him to do a complete halt and standstill, or to move toward the fence or away from it. This keeps him alert and listening for my cues. If the colt tries to outthink me or doesn't wait for my signal to tell him which maneuver I want him to perform, I'll either make him stop and stand, then stop and back, or I'll make him turn in the opposite direction from that in which he tried to turn—anything to change his mind and make him learn that he must wait for and obey my cues.

Spend five to ten minutes turning into the fence, turning away from the fence, or halting and waiting, three or four times a week, and you should begin to see an improvement in your colt's level of responsiveness. Do not ask in any set pattern or you will lose the benefit of this exercise, which is to teach your colt to wait for the rider's cues. Asking in a set routine will cause the colt to perform by habit. If you always turn into the fence, the colt will think, "Walk down the fence. Halt. Walk. Turn toward the fence and walk in the other direction."

CHANGE YOUR ROUTINE

Do not ask the colt to change directions in the same place every time or he will always try to turn and change direction in that same spot. He will be halting or trying to turn in a specific place rather than waiting for your cues.

USE THE SERPENTINE

Another useful exercise is to serpentine back and forth across your arena. Start at one end, turn first left and then right, left and right, until you come to the end of the arena, where you must reverse the sequence. This exercise also teaches a colt to travel in a straight line without depending on the fence as you travel across the middle of the arena. Use your rein and leg cues to make the colt travel straight. If he tries to veer to the left, effectively correct him by making him go twice as far to the right. Show him that it is to his benefit to travel in a straight line. If you ask the colt to stop in the center of the arena, and he tries to turn right before he stops, make him turn twice as far to the left before you allow him to stop. Show him that he must listen to and obey your cues.

I also use the serpentine exercise a lot on colts that are headed for careers as hunters or English pleasure horses, to teach them to extend their trot. When traveling the long, straight line, I ask them to extend their trot. When I approach the corner, I ask them to slow down. I make the corner at a posting trot and then ask again for an extended trot across the arena.

Using the long side of the arena gives the colt room to build up to a suitable speed at the extended trot. You may also do this same exercise in a large, flat field. Doing this same exercise on a Western horse will teach him to travel in a straight line without the benefit of a fence. Jog across the arena, ask the colt to walk to make the turn, then jog to the other side. As he becomes proficient at this, ask him to lope across the arena, jog the corner, and lope again. It doesn't hurt Western horses to learn to extend their trot on command.

CANTER OR LOPE

Advance to asking your colt to canter or lope circles half the size of your arena. After he has loped two or three circles, bring him down to a jog or trot, cross the center line, and canter or lope in the opposite direction. Be sure to not always lope the same number of circles before you cross the arena. Your colt must learn that he must wait for and obey your cues. Another time, jog or trot across the center of the pen and ask the colt to

Performing a lope-to-walk transition, then rewarding the colt from time to time, helps to keep him sharp.

I ask the colt to serpentine to keep him paying attention. In the initial stages, I apply the neck-rein cue as I turn, as well as the direct-rein cue.

halt and stand quietly. Reverse at a walk, and canter or lope circles on that same half of the ring but in the opposite direction.

Always vary your routine so that the colt doesn't learn to anticipate. If he does begin to anticipate your next command, change what you had in mind. Make him go right if he tries to go left, and left if he tries to go right. Make him wait for your command. Be sure that you don't inadvertently tell your colt to change before you "technically" ask for it by your body language. Often, a rider will shorten the reins before asking for a canter or lope. The colt learns to canter or lope on the shortening of the reins, rather than waiting for the rider to cue with his leg. Pay attention to what you are telling your colt. Every move that you make should mean something!

THINK BEFORE YOU RIDE

If you are going to train your horse, you must put the time into thinking where he needs work. Maybe one side is stiffer than the other or one gait is weaker than another. Or maybe he is giving you a problem with a certain segment of training; for example, turning left, picking up a lope or canter, or halting squarely. Riding and training a colt is as much a mental process as it is a physical one. Watch your colt as he gallops freely through your pasture and think of how you can best tell him to perform that way under saddle.

Horses tell us so much if only we take the time to "listen" and "think" before we "talk" to them. Be careful of what you say to your colt. Keep him attentive and waiting for your next command. Vary your routine, change your direction, and change your gaits often as your colt gains in understanding of these new mounted maneuvers. Show a colt that not only must he walk, jog/trot, or lope/canter on the rail, he must also obey your commands to cross the arena, go forward on a trail, and basically do *as* you ask, *when* you ask.

I've asked the colt to halt and back up.

CHAPTER FIFTEEN

The First Trail Ride

◆

If your lessons advance to a point where your colt readily obeys your cues to halt, turn left, turn right and go forward on command, he should be ready for his first trail ride. With a quiet, willing colt, you may be ready to hit the trail in a few weeks. With a skittish colt (one that spooks at every little noise or new sight), you are better off staying in the arena until he shows his willingness to obey your commands readily. Let him learn to trust that you will not put him in a situation that will hurt him. Taking a skittish colt out of the confines of the arena too soon can let him learn bad habits—habits that he might never have started if you had stayed in the arena an extra month or so. With any colt, it is best to never let him learn that he can get away with things like refusing to go forward, spinning and bolting toward home, bucking, or rearing.

An untrained colt faced with a spooky obstacle before he completely understands that he must obey you without question will find that spinning and running toward home "saves" him from the scary obstacle. And it perhaps scares you enough so that you will not take him past that scary obstacle again. A colt that is more solid in his training will obey your commands, especially the whoa command, without question. He understands that he must obey you.

For your first trail ride out of the arena, ask a friend who has a quiet, confident, well-mannered trail horse to ride with you. That will give your colt confidence and a horse to follow, if he becomes hesitant about crossing the wide-open spaces or certain obstacles.

KEEP YOUR FIRST RIDE SHORT

Plan your first ride to be a short one—twenty minutes to an hour, depending on your colt's fitness level, the ease of the trail, and your colt's level of training. Traveling up and down hills will take more out of your colt than working in a flat, sand-covered arena. Don't push for too much too soon. Trail riding should be enjoyable for the colt. Don't push him past what he is capable of giving at this point in time.

This is usually the time when a colt will begin to act up. He may find new tricks that you could prevent by giving him more time to develop the proper muscles. Remember that a colt must learn to balance your weight over obstacles, up and down hills, and on uneven terrain. This is all a new experience for him. Take your time and let him develop the proper muscles as well as learn slowly. Don't push for too much, too soon. Let the colt build up the proper amount of conditioning under saddle before you take longer rides.

Ride with another horse, both leading and following.

It is important to ride with a companion the first time, and it is a good practice to continue until your colt becomes solid at obeying your cues. Riding with a companion is more enjoyable and safer. If your colt spooks or refuses to go forward while he is in front, he will generally follow an older, more settled horse past a new or scary obstacle. If you get into any kind of trouble, a helper may save the day and turn what could have been a disaster into just another trail ride.

When riding with another horse, try to keep at least one horse length between horses. At faster gaits, increase the distance between horses. This is sometimes difficult to do on a young horse. You may want to ride the first few times on a dirt road where you may ride to the side of the other horse. This way you will not have to pull on your colt's mouth to try to constantly keep him off the other horse's tail. If your colt is a faster walker than the other horse, let your colt lead if he is willing. Teach him to lead and to follow.

KEEP A SAFE DISTANCE

Keeping a safe distance between horses allows you time to stop if you see the horse in front of you falter or halt. A handy trick learned years ago is for the lead rider to raise his right hand when he is slowing from one gait to another. This gives the rider in back time to slow his horse without running into the horse in front. If every rider in the group raises a hand as soon as he sees the signal to slow down, it can be passed down the line. In this way, you'll avoid a pile-up of horses at the beginning of the line, which could be dangerous, especially on a young horse.

Most young horses are intimidated by older horses. When caught in a group, they tend to act as they do in a pasture and will try to avoid a more aggressive type of horse. It takes time for a young horse to learn that the rules of the pasture change once horses are mounted. It will take time for a young horse to learn to trust that you can keep him safe from a more aggressive horse when all are under saddle. He must learn that he doesn't have to turn tail and run if an older horse threatens him. These are things that happen with a young horse, and it is best if you can perceive the situation from the colt's point of view. He's spent two years in a pasture being low man on the totem pole, and now he must learn that humans are higher up on the pole and all horses must obey humans.

RIDE CONFIDENTLY

When riding the trails and approaching an obstacle, either in front or following, don't "tell" your colt through your body language that he should be afraid. If you tense *your* body, your colt will feel *your* fear. That may be enough to make him suspicious of crossing an obstacle. When you see an obstacle approaching, continue to breathe deeply, keep your colt's head pointed straight forward, and slightly squeeze both legs on his sides to tell him that he must continue to go straight ahead. Do not give him any indication through your body language that you are afraid of his reaction to the obstacle. Horses have been negotiating logs and streams for years without falling or breaking a leg. Sit quietly. Give your colt enough rein to drop his nose and look at the obstacle, yet not so much rein that he can spin or bolt. Keep his head pointed straight forward. Let him pick the best way through the obstacle.

Keep a rein in each hand when crossing an obstacle so that you may direct the colt, keeping his nose pointed straight ahead.

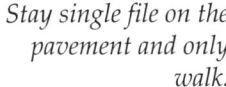

Stay single file on the pavement and only walk.

If your colt tries to avoid an obstacle, because he is afraid to step over a log or walk over a ditch, let the more experienced horse go first so that your colt can see that there is nothing to be afraid of. In most instances, your colt will easily follow a seasoned horse over an obstacle.

When approaching water or other obstacles that may be scary to your colt, ride with one rein in each hand. Keep each hand about eight inches to either side of the saddle horn. In this way, you can keep your colt's head "between your hands" and pointed straight forward. If your colt turns his nose to the left, use your right rein to direct his head back to a straight-ahead position, and vice versa. If he tips his nose and you do not correct it, his body will soon follow. By keeping his head pointed in the direction that you wish to go and squeezing or bumping with your legs, you can send the colt forward over the obstacle.

If you approach a log across the trail, your colt has one of two options. He may choose to step over it or he may jump it. After a few obstacles, you'll have a good idea how your colt will approach such hazards. If your colt chooses to carefully step over an obstacle, you must give him his head so that he can judge where to place his feet. If he chooses to jump it, jumping on the trail is the same as jumping in a ring, even if your colt is tacked Western. Lean forward slightly as you approach the jump, giving him enough rein so that as he jumps you will not inadvertently pull on his mouth as he stretches his neck. He must stretch or extend his neck to balance going over a jump. If you are unsure of your jumping abilities, hold the horn or a handful of mane. This will keep you from falling backwards as he thrusts off with his hind feet. As a long-time instructor, I'd prefer to see a student hold the mane or the horn rather than jerk on an unsuspecting horse that has done nothing wrong going over a jump.

After a few obstacles, you'll have an idea how your colt generally reacts to obstacles lying on or over the trail. In either case, it is best to be prepared. While a colt may almost always walk or pick his way over an obstacle, on certain hazards he may prefer to jump. Be prepared! A colt will come to fear certain obstacles if he gets banged in the mouth every time he tries to pop over one. If all else fails, and he refuses to cross an obstacle, dismount and lead him across. However, remember that horses, especially young ones, may be worried or afraid. They may jump even if you dismount. Always stand to the side because a young horse may jump into you. Give him enough rein to jump the obstacle without hurting himself or you, or banging his mouth as he lands.

Walking on a rocky section of the trail should be treated as another obstacle. Give the colt his head and let him choose where to put his feet. Let him pick the best way—unless, of course, it becomes dangerous. A colt that is a little sore-footed may choose to walk on the edge of a rocky trail where the ground is softer. As long as there are no branches in your way, let him walk where he chooses. If he seems sore, it is probably time to put shoes and/or pads on your colt or invest in a pair of "Easy Boots."

Don't pick a rocky point in the trail to lope or gallop. A stone bruise (made when the horse's hoof hits a rock too hard, the wrong way) can take time to heal. This will interfere with your riding time. Save your jogging and loping for a clear spot on the trail and let the colt walk through the rocky sections.

RIDING UPHILL

Some colts will jog up a hill the first few times they are faced with negotiating one. When riding up a steep incline, either at a walk or jog, stand slightly in your stirrups, grab a handful of mane halfway up the colt's neck, and lean forward. Getting off of the colt's back frees his hindquarters so that he can better propel himself up the hill. To ride downhill, do the opposite. Your center of gravity should stay over the horse's center. When going downhill, lean slightly back to compensate for the decline. Most declines should be ridden at a walk. Your colt will appreciate these small kindnesses that make his job easier.

If a limb is hanging in the path, ask the rider in front of you to lift the limb up and over his head as he passes under it. This will keep the limb from snapping back in your colt's face and spooking him. Some colts will spook at a slightly moving branch or limb, so be prepared. If your colt has been quiet and you can move around in the saddle without spooking him, lean down on his neck so that you can go under the limb or lift the limb up and ride under it. Be prepared for your colt to react. This may be a new experience for him and might cause him to bolt or spook.

DISMOUNTING ON THE TRAIL

If, during the course of your trail ride, you must stop and dismount, all horses should stop. Wait until everybody is back in the saddle before you move off down the trail. It can be difficult to keep a young horse standing still to mount if the rest of the horses move off down the trail. Horses are herd animals and like to stay together. Be courteous. Wait until everyone is mounted and ready to ride before the lead horse begins. On the same note, if a rider falls or a horse runs away, all horses should stop and wait for the rider to regain control. Running after a spooked colt will only cause the horse to become more nervous and will make him run faster, especially on his first trail ride.

BEWARE OF TRAFFIC

When leaving a trail and approaching a paved road, always look first for oncoming traffic. Be prepared for your colt to spook the first time or two that he sees a car whizzing toward him. Do not let him stand with his nose pointed across the street because he may bolt right into the car. Position him so that he is facing to the left or right. This way, if he does bolt, you can turn him back toward the trail or onto the side of the road.

Walk in the direction of the traffic. Stay single file so that cars may pass you. Keep the quiet, older horse in front of you to prevent your colt from bolting up the road. If necessary (and if you know that the other horse will not kick), you can force your colt directly behind that horse. That is better than letting your colt race uncontrollably up the road. If you hear a car coming that is going too fast, try to signal for him to slow down. Colts are unpredictable, and you never know how they might react. While you shouldn't take an unruly colt on a road traveled by cars, a colt must be taught to deal with traffic at some point in his life.

Never jog or lope on pavement because there is no "give" to it. The concussion can create havoc with the bones and ligaments in your colt's legs, sometimes doing irreparable damage. Keep your colt to a walk and wait for the soft ground of the trails to jog or lope.

Contact your county extension office or look for detailed maps with available trails marked. There may be a state forest nearby where you can ride. You can introduce your colt to the trails without fear of dealing with traffic. Asking at nearby barns is another source of information. If you have a trailer, you can truck your colt to the trails and avoid many of the paved roads, teaching your colt to trailer as well.

With each trail ride, your colt should become a more obedient and willing partner in your travels. Remember that while trail rides are fun for both humans and horses, you should still expect your colt to be obedient to your commands. Trail riding is a nice break from ring work, but it should not be cause for

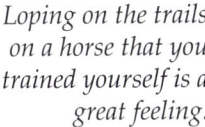

Loping on the trails on a horse that you trained yourself is a great feeling.

him to learn bad habits. Ask, tell, then enforce your commands to behave on the trail just as you do in the ring. The more trails that you ride on, the better he should become. What once caused him to spook should eventually be taken in stride and passed with hardly a glance. Never forget that you are on 1,000 pounds of power that can be totally unpredictable. Expect the unexpected. Most of all, enjoy the new experiences—your first trail ride with a colt that you trained, walking ten feet from a newborn fawn, traveling on trails inaccessible by motor vehicle, and riding the wide-open spaces of nature.

Mostly, it takes time—hours spent in the saddle on the trail—to train a colt to be a good trail horse. Starting with a good, sensible colt that is not easily spooked and that heeds your basic commands will make the process a lot smoother. A colt that seems bored with work in the ring can become a new horse when he is faced with being the leader on a leisurely trail ride.

TRAIN ON THE TRAIL

Be sure to make your colt respond to your cues when he needs direction and let him pick his way and enjoy himself when he is performing correctly. Walk the first mile out (to warm up your colt's muscles) and the last mile home (to cool him down).

Trail riding is enjoyable for both horse and rider.

Crossing Water

———— ◆ ————

Imagine that you are riding your colt along a quiet, woodsy trail enjoying the sounds of nature. The colt's hoofbeats are muffled by fallen pine needles, the silence broken only by an occasional twig that snaps beneath his feet. You round a bend in the trail and suddenly he stops—a large stream or body of water is in his path. With a toss of his head, he rears and spins, headed back in the direction from which he just came.

Will you be able to "make" your colt cross the water? Or must you turn back and reroute your ride to find a bridge? Will your colt cross a bridge? Or must you return home, the day marred by the unwillingness of your colt to cross water?

Crossing water seems to be one of the most difficult obstacles for a horse to learn to negotiate. Be prepared to work calmly with him for as long as it takes to let him learn that crossing water is just one more obstacle on the trail.

Choose your spot to cross water the first time with care. Look for shallow water with good footing, not a raging stream like you might find after a thunderstorm. Try to avoid a steep drop before the water, which sometimes happens when the water level is low. Start with an easy, shallow stream. Then, as your colt gains confidence, gradually build to crossing larger or deeper streams.

Use this three-step program, plus alternate methods for the extremely water-shy colt, to train your colt to cross water without a fuss. These same methods can also be used for bridges, ditches or other obstacles.

Some colts will cross a large stream the first time they encounter one. Other times, a colt may balk at crossing water on your initial rides, only to change his mind a few months later and willingly cross water with seemingly no additional training from you. Why?

STEP 1: TEACH HIM TO TRUST YOUR JUDGMENT

Before a colt will willingly carry you over an obstacle, he must trust you. Show your colt that you will not ask for more than he is capable of giving. Never over-extend or overface your colt. Never put your colt in a situation where he can get hurt; this will put him back months in training time. Pushing a tired colt past his ability or fitness level can cause injuries to muscles, tendons, and/or ligaments. This, in turn, can cause a colt to become sour, resentful, or wary of giving you his trust. The most successful training method is one that includes a gradual buildup, step by step, on what the colt already knows, as well as building his fitness level in a proper manner. Teaching a colt to trust you can have significant, lasting results beyond just teaching him to cross water. A colt must trust you and also obey your go-forward cues.

STEP 2: GO FORWARD

The basis of all training is for a colt to go forward on your cues. A colt must understand that when you "tell" him to go forward, he must obey, whether it be for a leisurely jog around the arena, negotiating a course of fences when he becomes a suitable age, or crossing water on the trail. This training begins in the ring and carries over to any and all other work, both inside and outside the ring.

Any time that a colt stops and doesn't obey your go-forward cues, his training is regressing a step. If a colt learns that

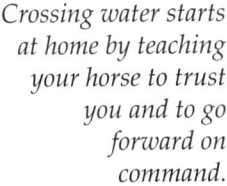

Crossing water starts at home by teaching your horse to trust you and to go forward on command.

he can ignore your go-forward cues, you are headed for a fight. It is important to win the fight before it becomes a major battle, or the day may come that your colt will refuse to go forward at all.

To correct a colt that will not go forward, exaggerate your cues or use increasingly stronger cues until he responds. As soon as the colt begins to move forward, immediately stop using any and all go-forward cues to reward him. If the colt stops again, repeat the procedure, being sure to cease your cues as soon as he moves forward. Timing is essential.

Go-forward cues, listed in order of severity, can include: squeezing with your calves, bumping with your heels, making your colt walk in small circles so that he learns it is easier to obey your go-forward cues than it is to consistently walk in small circles, tapping from a crop behind the girth, or using spurs if you have a secure lower leg.

This doesn't mean that if your colt refuses to cross a stream the first time he encounters one, you must force him to cross it. Turn the situation around so that you look like the winner, at least in the colt's mind. Horses are not dumb, by any means, but they can be baffled by an enterprising person. Use this to your advantage. Never let the colt think that you want him to cross water that day if you have not prepared for a water crossing on a balky colt. Never let a battle start. Stay relaxed and ask the colt to change directions. Make it be *your* idea not to go close to the water on that day. Ride some circles and ride back and forth before the stream, making sure that the colt turns in the direction that *you* choose (the opposite direction from that which the colt chooses). This reinforces to the colt that he must heed your cues. Do this long enough to take his mind off of the water crossing and to reestablish your authority. Change the focus of the trip from crossing water to a mini-schooling session of lessons that he performs well. Try not to punish a colt by water or he may think that water is a dangerous or an unfriendly place to be.

If your colt gives you a problem with crossing water, and you are not prepared to make him cross water, change the focus of your trip to a mini-schooling session so that the colt doesn't think that he won.

By refusing to cross water, the colt may be telling you that he is afraid, but he is also telling you that he has no trust of your judgment and no respect for your go-forward cues. Go home and prepare yourself and your colt. Pick another day to specifically train the colt to cross water at a proper "first-time" crossing. Come back with a seasoned horse that will cross water. Ask the seasoned horse to cross water while you follow behind. Many colts will follow another horse across water if you ride confidently and do not tell the colt through your body language that you are afraid.

STEP 3: BEWARE OF YOUR BODY LANGUAGE

If you are afraid, the colt will feel it and think that he should be afraid. Many water-crossing problems are caused by lack of rider confidence. The colt feels that you aren't entirely sure that you want to cross the water. Therefore, the colt thinks that since you aren't entirely sure, there is no reason why he should cross the water. This is similar to jumping fences. As the saying goes, "Throw your heart over the jump (or the water crossing) and the horse will follow."

I've proven this theory to my fellow riders a number of times. I can be on the youngest, the most timid, and/or the least water-wise colt of the group, yet can lead an entire group of horses across a stream. Granted, I probably have more experience on more types of horses than the people with whom I ride but it comes down to riding confidently. Never let a colt feel that he should doubt the wisdom of your judgment. Horses rely on body language. They can "hear" what you are "saying," loud and clear, if you are tense or afraid.

The next time you feel your colt hesitating, say to yourself, over and over, "We are going to cross this stream. I am not afraid. I know that my colt can safely cross this stream."

POINT HIS NOSE ACROSS THE STREAM

Point your colt's nose at the other side of the stream and urge him on. Hold your reins, one in each hand, keeping his head between the bridle. Keep his head pointed straight forward. Using two hands on the reins makes it easier to guide the colt in a straight line. Pretend that this is just another stretch of trail, which is really all it is. Your colt should have learned to obey your go-forward cues from prior training and should know that you would not ask him to cross if it was unsafe. Sit relaxed, yet alert. Ride confidently. Give the colt no reason to doubt your judgment or the fact that you want him to cross the water now. If you are hesitant about going over the stream, the colt will feel it and will be hesitant to cross.

Find a clear, shallow spot to cross. Keep his nose pointed straight ahead with a rein in each hand, and tell him to cross.

Beware. Some horses like to paw. This may be followed by a roll.

If you have a very timid colt, following a lead horse across the stream the first few times until you both gain confidence is the best idea. Sit quietly and urge your colt forward after the other horse. Take deep breaths. Don't tense or tighten your muscles because that tells your colt that you are afraid. Bear in mind that some may hesitate briefly on one side, then rush in after the other horse. Be careful not to jerk on the colt's mouth if this happens because he will feel that you are punishing him for crossing. You may pick up light contact and ask him to walk across in a mannerly fashion, but be sure not to jerk on his mouth or punish him for crossing.

A word of caution: At some point in his training, a colt may decide that he likes water. If your colt starts to paw, be forewarned that he may try to roll. Lift your reins to lift his head (if he paws) and urge him across the water. It does happen—pay attention.

THE PROBLEM HORSE

If your colt absolutely refuses to cross water, even when following a lead horse, you may be able to coax him through a shallow stream if you lead him from the ground. I don't recommend doing this unless you are an experienced horse person. If you must resort to this method, try to lead your colt in first, rather than follow the lead horse. Once your colt's feet are in the water, mount right there and ride him across. If he won't go into the water, have the lead horse walk in partway. Try to walk your colt next to the lead horse, being sure that you are not in the middle of the two horses. Never let the lead horse get too far ahead of you. An insecure colt, frantic over being left behind, may leap right into you, knocking you down and possibly landing on top of you.

Another option is to pony the water-shy colt across a stream. This will expose him to water without a rider on his back. If you have the experience to handle two horses, this may be a bit safer than leading a colt from the ground, if you have first taught the colt to accept being ponied from another horse.

If these methods fail, or if you prefer to teach your colt to cross water without being on his back, put him in a pasture where he has to cross water. Make sure that he has to cross by placing his hay or grain on the opposite side from where he is standing. Once a colt crosses water on his own in a pasture, ride him confidently across that same crossing before advancing to different and varied crossings.

START SMALL

Be fair to your colt. Do not expect him to cross a very wide or deep stream or river without first negotiating smaller, shallower crossings to gain confidence. You may have to wait for the summer sun (or drought) to lower the water level, but waiting for the proper time will pay off in the long run.

Take the time to train your colt to cross water in a slow, confident manner. Nothing is more disheartening than watching your buddies continue their ride across a stream as you wave from the other side, forced to return home because of a colt that refuses (or has not been taught how) to cross water. You wouldn't expect your colt to run a reining pattern or jump a fence without proper training. Don't expect him to cross water without training, particularly if he's never had to cross a stream before because he lives in a dry paddock.

If your colt absolutely refuses to cross water, pay a trainer to teach your colt that water is a harmless obstacle. Your safety is worth the price of a month's training.

CROSSING BRIDGES, GULLIES AND DITCHES

Bridges, gullies, and ditches are other obstacles that sometimes cause a young horse to become frightened. Follow the same basic program to teach your colt that it is safe to cross. Hold a rein each hand, keeping him between the bridle, and urge him forward with your legs. Be sure to ride with a companion horse that is confident. Two horses rearing or spinning before a bridge or gully is not a pretty sight. Someone can get hurt. If you do lead your horse across, watch that he doesn't jump into you, looking for safety as he would with his dam.

Teaching Your Horse To Jump

◆

eaching a colt to jump should not be done until he is at least three years of age (and then only over very small jumps or cavelletti). Preferably, you'll wait until your colt is four or five years old. You can introduce your two-year-old to poles on the ground, teaching him to walk and then trot over them confidently, after he has learned to balance your weight and has learned basic control. This will begin to prepare him for a future career as a hunter or jumper.

You can show your colt different types of jumps. Trot around the jumps set in your arena, circling and serpentining through them. This will teach the colt basic obedience and help to stretch his side muscles as he bends and weaves through the jumps. Drop the poles to the ground so that you may trot through the standards, either those set up in your arena or out on the hunt course, once he has proven to be controllable outside of the arena.

A three-year-old can be taught some of the basics of jumping—the flat work that will later help him over fences, raised poles, cavelletti, and the infrequent small fence. This will give you a chance to evaluate his future potential as a hunter or jumper. A three-year-old can be longed over small fences from time to time allowing you to evaluate his natural form or ability. But a three-year-old is not physically ready to jump higher fences. A young horse that is pushed too soon will not stay sound as will the horse that is started later.

I'll give you my basic program for starting a horse over fences. Adjust it to your colt's age, or wait until he is of an age to jump. Ninety percent of a jumping course is flat work, and that is something that you can begin to polish as soon as a colt understands the concept of going forward on command, turning left, turning right, and halting.

KNOWING THE BASICS

Before you start to jump any horse, the horse must know the basics. He should walk, trot, and canter at a consistent pace with the tempo or beat the same. You should be able to collect and extend the horse's gait as needed, both at the trot and at the canter. You can start now teaching your colt the cues needed to move his hips and shoulders to meet the center of each fence. This will only help later when the colt is of an age to jump higher fences. Correctness is important. By taking the time now, the colt will have the solid background that he needs in order to jump higher fences later.

ACCEPTING A POLE ON THE GROUND

As you start to school over poles and then fences, remember to start slowly and gain the horse's trust. Your first lesson introduces the horse to a pole on the ground. Walk and trot over the pole until the horse accepts it. If the horse rushes it, leaps over it, shies at it, or in any way tells you that he has not accepted it calmly, don't go any farther. Continue walking and trotting over a pole on the ground until the horse no longer fears it or tries to rush over it. His pace must stay consistent with the tempo or beat the same. This is the basis for all future lessons.

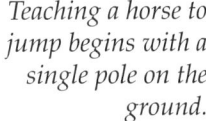

Teaching a horse to jump begins with a single pole on the ground.

RAISE THE POLE

As the horse's pace becomes consistent over a pole on the ground, raise it to six inches. Trot over the raised pole until your horse's pace again stays consistent. If he rushes over a pole on the ground, he will rush over a fence. Show him that there is nothing to fear and no reason to rush. Teach him that his lesson won't end any sooner if he goes faster rather than slower.

Vary your routine by circling or approaching the pole from different directions. You can use more than one pole placed at various intervals throughout your schooling area and incorporate these raised poles with your schooling on the flat. This will help to keep both you and your horse from becoming bored.

ADD A POLE

When the horse's pace stays consistent with one raised pole, add another pole four feet away. Check to see that the horse can stride comfortably through the poles, one step between each pole. (The poles may need to be adjusted for different horses.) Wait until you feel the horse relax with this step before you go any farther.

As the horse becomes comfortable with two raised poles, ask him to trot through four or five raised poles, each the same distance apart. Trot fifteen or twenty feet past the last pole and halt squarely. This will teach the horse obedience. Loosen your reins and sit for a minute or so when he trots the line correctly to reward the horse. Never loosen your reins so much that you have no control if the horse decides to spook or run off. Safety for you, as the rider, is the greatest concern.

Set your cavelletti so that the horse can stride comfortably through them.

Only when he trots through your line of raised poles at a steady, consistent pace should you go on to the next step. Let the *horse* dictate the speed of the training program.

ADD A CROSS-RAIL

Next, add a cross-rail seven feet after the four raised poles. Start with it very low, and only raise it after the horse trots through this line at a consistent pace. The horse should start the line to the raised poles in a straight line and finish after the last cross-rail in a straight line. Work on control and correctness. Don't let the horse cut corners, either before or at the end of the line. Keep him traveling straight to the center of the fence.

Be sure to soften your hands as your horse goes over a fence. This allows the horse to use his head and neck as a balancing tool without fear of getting popped in the mouth.

WATCH YOUR HANDS

As the rider, make sure that you are not telling the horse that something spooky or scary is coming up by tensing your body. Also, don't look down at the fence. That will weight the horse's forehand, throw your horse off-balance, and cause a crash when you advance to bigger fences. Pick a center point after the fence and keep your eyes up. If you think that your horse will pop over a fence (and you might grab his mouth), add a neck strap and take hold of it ten feet before the jump. The worst thing that you can do is bang a horse's mouth going over a fence. This can easily cause a horse to dislike jumping and become fearful or resentful. It is also a reason why some horses rush fences—they think that by going faster, they can get over the fence faster to avoid the pain that they associate with jumping.

For your next lesson, put four raised poles at each corner of the ring. Trot a figure-eight pattern over these poles. (Your figure-eight pattern will look like two square circles that meet in the centers.) Approach each raised pole in a straight line as you would a fence. Always aim for the center. Go over the pole and

Look up.

continue straight away before making a quarter turn to cross the center of the ring. Then make another quarter turn to approach the next raised pole, again in a straight line.

TEACH OBEDIENCE

Teach obedience. Make the horse respond and respect your aids. Use this time to teach your horse to approach and leave the fence in a straight line and to also continue between poles at your chosen speed. Use these poles on the ground until your horse will trot this "course" obediently.

By beginning with the basics and jumping raised poles, rather than fences, you can work on your horse's speed or pace control, his consistency, and meeting each fence in the center without stress to his legs from jumping. Concentrate now on any other problems that may arise, such as traveling straight to a fence or bending around the corners correctly. Remember that a small problem over a pole on the ground becomes a big problem over a three-foot fence. Use this training time to your advantage. Fix any problems that arise, before adding height and/or increasing the degree of difficulty by changing distances between each fence.

Once your colt is a three-year-old, you can begin with these lessons, always keeping the cross-rails very low. Don't work on jumping a three-year-old more than once or twice a week. Keep your lessons short. Aim for obedience and correctness. Jumping higher fences when he is older will be a breeze if you can successfully negotiate small cross-rails now.

For his next lesson, put four cavelletti or poles in a row, raised to six inches, followed by one cross-rail seven feet away (room for landing and takeoff). Add a second cross-rail nine feet away. Trot the raised poles, then squeeze to ask for the jump, and jump again. This is a bounce fence—no stride in between each fence. Halt the horse on a straight line after the last fence. Don't let him rush off after the last fence—he must wait for your next command. Make him respect your aids and wait until you tell him to move off.

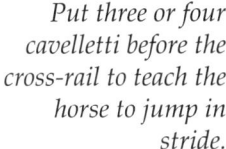

Put three or four cavelletti before the cross-rail to teach the horse to jump in stride.

BUILD TRUST

Work with these small cross-rails to build trust in the horse. He must know that you will not put him in a situation that will hurt him. Never overface a horse by jumping too large too soon.

Now change the bounce fence to an in and out. Move the second cross-rail eighteen to twenty-four feet away from the first fence. This way, the horse will jump in, take one canter stride, and jump out. Again, ask him to halt in a straight line after the last fence. If he has to reach to meet the second fence, move it closer. If he gets in too close, move it farther away. Play with the distances until you find what works for your horse. Make it easy for him now. Later, when the horse is more experienced and he trusts you, you can make these distances shorter or longer to increase the degree of difficulty.

You can go back to this gymnastic line at any point in your training. You can add fences and jump three or four small bounce fences in a row when the horse is older. This will teach him to round his back and to bring his hocks underneath himself. But don't overdo it. Four or five times through a line like this is enough per lesson. This is hard work for a horse—even for an older horse.

To begin to practice riding a course, set up a "course" using just the standards (no rails between them). Trot the "course." Insist on precision and correctness. Approach each set of standards in a straight line and ride through the exact center. This is just more flat work. Your horse should respond willingly and show no signs of resentment. Spend as many days as necessary until you can trot and then canter through these standards, taking the corners correctly and meeting each "fence" at the center. Once the horse goes through this "course" easily, make each jump a small cross-rail. Ride this "new" course jumping the small cross-rails. When your horse will calmly negotiate this course, raise the cross-rails to twelve- or eighteen-inch verticals.

As your horse ages, and all is going well, slowly begin adding height to your fences. If your horse rushes or in any way tries to avoid a particular fence, back up a step. Change the fence to a cross-rail, jump it at a trot, and then at a canter. Show the horse that there is nothing to fear.

Never reward a horse for rushing or avoiding fences by dismounting and putting him away. Drop the pole to the ground if you have to and trot him over it. Then raise it to a small cross-rail or vertical. If he jumps correctly, stop him, dismount, and put him away. This tells the horse that he did as you asked and he is being rewarded.

Practice approaching jumps in a straight line, and ending in a straight line.

Think of how the horse may interpret your actions. If you continue schooling over and over a jump that the horse has jumped correctly, he will wonder why you are punishing him (by forcing him over the pole or fence again and again). Tell him that he has done it the right way by letting him rest for a minute or going on to another fence or other flat work.

In the same respect, if he rushes a fence or refuses one, and you continue (even at a lower height) until he jumps it correctly, he will understand that he does not go back to the barn until he jumps correctly. Reward good behavior and correct bad behavior.

On some days, ride to your course after you have finished your flat work and jump only one or two easy fences. Then put him away. Change his mind. Let him know that every time he sees a course of fences, he won't have to put in an all-out effort.

Learn to go with the horse. Don't throw your reins away as you approach a fence. You will then have no control over the horse or where he goes. If you are not ready to follow his head, use a crest release or a neck strap.

SOFTEN YOUR HANDS

As the horse gets close to the fence, remember to soften your hands. This allows the horse to use his head and neck to get over the fence. (The head and neck are a balancing tool for the horse.) By softening your hands and going with him, you give the horse the freedom to use himself to get over the fence. Don't interfere with him or pull on his mouth. Make jumping an enjoyable experience for him.

Always train in a logical, sequential manner. This not only teaches the horse correctly, it also develops the proper muscles. Set your distances correctly to build confidence and to teach the horse to meet each fence correctly. As he becomes experienced, you may then add lines with different, difficult distances. For now, make it easy. Work on getting precision in your flat work to get precision in your jumping. You need impulsion, not speed, and a steady pace to jump correctly.

When training, set both yourself and your horse up for success. Make it easy for the horse to do as you ask. By starting with the basics and building on them, you show your horse that jumping can be enjoyable.

Teaching a horse to jump is a long process. Have patience and go slowly. The time you spend now will pay dividends in the future. Work on getting a steady, consistent pace between fences. Practice putting your horse to the center of each fence in preparation for bigger fences later. Polish your approach and your landing so that when you begin to jump higher fences, your horse has the confidence to take them in stride.

When you set up a course to jump, always make the first fence the most inviting and the easiest—a warmup for the horse. The middle fences should build up to the hardest, and the end lets them down. The last fence should be as easy as the first one. This is good for your horse's mental attitude—one more way to keep the horse happy and enjoying his work. Take your time now so that when you get to higher fences, your horse will take them in stride, both mentally and physically.

CHAPTER EIGHTEEN

Conditioning, Worming, and Vaccines

◆

Your colt has spent his first two to three years playing, growing and learning how to be a horse. He's probably had only a limited amount of longeing or other physical work prior to being saddle broken. Once he is of an age to saddle break, remember that he needs to be brought along slowly to increase his fitness level. His level of condition must change from that of a pre-riding level to that of a lightly used saddle horse. Don't overwork a two-year-old colt, although he can certainly be taught the basics of riding. Plan the length and type of your lessons to correspond with your colt's age and physical ability.

Not only will his muscle tone need to be increased slowly, the skin on his back where the saddle and girth lie will need time to toughen up. Much as your hands become callused to a certain degree through work, a colt's back must toughen to carry a saddle for a long period of time. Because of a colt's limited attention span, I only ride for thirty to forty-five minutes during the initial training. This allows the colt to develop the mental attitude needed to begin a career under saddle, and it gives his back time to toughen up.

USING A BREAST COLLAR

I like to use a breast collar on the colts that I start under saddle because it helps to keep the saddle in position. You do not have to tighten the girth quite as much, but be careful. A fleece-lined, web/felt or neoprene girth is better than a string girth. String girths seem to rub more and create sores. Most colts have round backs and have not yet developed withers, so there's not much to keep the saddle in place.

BE SURE THAT THE SADDLE FITS

Be sure that the saddle fits your colt. There are books on the subject, although it is best to ask a knowledgeable person in your area. I look for a tree that fits the colt's back and doesn't pinch, one that doesn't rub on his "withers," and one that is not too large for a colt to wear. When your colt is sweating lightly, remove the saddle and look for dry spots left on his back where the saddle lies. If you see dry spots, or spots without sweat, it means that your saddle is too tight in that area. It is not allowing for proper circulation that will let the colt sweat evenly across his back. Change saddles or try different types of padding until you find one that fits your colt comfortably.

PLACE THE SADDLE ON GENTLY

Never drop the saddle on a colt's back and/or jerk up harshly on the girth to tighten it. If your colt is hard to catch or angers you in some other way before saddling, do not take it out on him when you put the saddle on his back. He has long forgotten about the chasing game that you played in the pasture and will have no way to associate your anger with saddling over his being hard to catch. Those are two totally different problems and must be treated as such. A colt soon learns that a saddle causes pain, and he will try to avoid what hurts him. If your normally quiet colt prances and dances in the cross-ties, or lays his ears back as you approach with the saddle, start looking to see where the problem lies. A colt will begin to dance and prance if you drop a saddle too harshly on his back or tighten the girth too quickly. He is trying to avoid being saddled. You may also see his back flinch as he thinks of the pain to come. Be sure that you place the saddle gently on his back and tighten the girth slowly, in increments.

Using a saddle that pinches the colt's back may cause him to buck. He may become one-sided—stiffer on one side than the other—or may refuse to work on one side at all. He may refuse to move forward. These problems are many times blamed on training errors when in fact the cause is a physical one. Putting a saddle too far forward on a colt's shoulders and cinching it down too tightly will cause problems, as will putting it too far back. Ask questions if there is the slightest bit of doubt in your mind.

START SLOWLY TO BUILD CONDITION

Once you are actually riding the colt, time your sessions, taking into consideration the amount of "speed" work you do—i.e. jogging/trotting or loping/cantering—as well as the temperature and humidity of the day. Don't ask the colt to overexert because his muscles will become sore. He needs to gain condition slowly. On the same note, rest from time to time so that he can catch his breath. Try to make riding a pleasant experience for a colt so that he doesn't become resentful over things that are easily under your control. Ride late at night when the sun is lower and the temperature cooler or earlier in the morning, before the temperature has risen. Sponge your colt's back with warm water if he is sweaty to rinse off the sweat. You don't want to turn him out with an itchy back. Rub him with a curry comb or brush him if the temperature is too cold to sponge him. A good brushing after a workout is something that all horses enjoy.

A relaxing trail ride in the shade of the woods is a good choice if it is hot as long as you first spray or sponge the colt with fly spray. Remember that you are building a good attitude as well as preparing the colt physically to carry you. Help him to be comfortable.

VACCINES

As you begin to ride your colt, the chances of him leaving the farm increase—to horse shows, on trail rides with other horses, etc.—so be sure that his vaccination schedule is up to date. On larger farms, where horses are coming in and out on a regular basis, this should be a matter of routine. On a small farm, or for a horse that lives in the backyard, certain vaccines may not have been recommended by your vet. But as you begin to work your colt and he leaves the farm more often, the chances of him being introduced to different viruses increase. Discuss what vaccines may be appropriate for your colt with your vet. He or she will know best what is prevalent in your area.

For a general recommendation, I suggest: Early in the year, January or February: tetanus, rabies, and a rhino/flu shot; in March or April: an encephalomyelitis vaccine and Potomac horse fever vaccine.

If this colt is headed for the show circuit, boosters of rhino/flu may be given every two to three months during the show season.

In the fall, September or early October, give a Potomac horse fever vaccine and perhaps a booster on the encephalomyelitis vaccine. Your vet is the best person to ask because he or she is familiar with your area. The cost of a vaccine is worth your colt's health.

WORMING

Worming is as important as vaccinating. This will depend somewhat on your specific conditions. A horse or colt that is kept alone with his paddock cleaned daily can get by with a limited amount of worming. A horse that is stabled in a place with many new or different horses coming in and out of his pasture should be wormed every month, especially if all new horses entering the herd are not dewormed. Young colts taste everything and are the most prone to picking up worms, yet older horses are susceptible as well. Worms can do serious internal damage, and the cost of a monthly tube of wormer is worth the price.

Wormers should be rotated. Use a different class of drug, not only just a new name brand. Read the label before you buy. I double-dose with Strongid P once a year (March or April) for tapeworms, unless I see the horse passing tapeworms in his manure. Then I double-dose again, as long as enough time has passed. When in doubt, call your vet. Tapeworms look like pieces of spaghetti. I use Ivermectrin once in January or February, once in the summer, and again in the fall. Consult your vet.

A fecal count of a fresh sample of the horse's manure can tell you if your worming program is effective or if it needs to be varied. There is usually only a small charge for this service— five or ten dollars. It is well worth the price, especially if your colt has that pot bellied, rough hair coat look to him that suggests a worm problem. Otherwise, a fecal count, done once a year, should help to keep your worming program on the right track.

The best way to prevent a worm problem is to keep your stalls and pens picked regularly. Keep your manure pile out of the pasture and at least 100 feet away from your barn. Never let your horses pick through the manure pile, as they will do to find a scrap of hay if they are hungry (and most horses think that they're always hungry, being programmed to eat twenty-three hours a day).

If you spread hay in the pasture for the horses to eat, be sure to avoid placing piles of hay by piles of manure or the horses will ingest worm eggs. A feeder, large enough for all horses to eat comfortably around, is a good idea, because you can clean around it. But be sure that all horses can get to the feeder to eat. Sometimes the more aggressive horses will chase the other horses (most notably the younger stock if pastured together), away from the choicest feed. You may think that you are feeding enough hay, but if one horse is not allowed to eat, he will lose weight. Remove any wet or moldy hay left in or around the feeder because it can cause respiratory problems.

Keep your stalls well ventilated yet draft-free. Be sure that your stalls are cleaned properly, with all wet spots removed and limed. The ammonia smell and accompanying bacteria from the urine and manure in the stall can create havoc with your horse's lungs as well as with his feet. Clean your stalls once or twice a day and rebed as needed.

CHOOSE YOUR FARRIER WITH CARE

Find a reputable farrier in your area. "No hoof, no horse." Never has a saying withstood the test of time better than that. Keep regular appointments, every six to eight weeks, depending on the time of year and your horse's type of hoof and actual hoof growth. If you plan to ride the trails and have mostly rocky ones in your area, put pads on now. This may keep your colt from getting a stone bruise. Clean your horse's feet on a daily basis and watch for thrush (hoof rot) whether he is shod or not.

Some colts that are ridden lightly may do all right without shoes, at least until their workload increases. Check with the farrier who has trimmed your colt up to this time. And your colt *should* have been trimmed regularly up to this time. Some leg problems can be corrected, but only if the colt is worked on at a very early age—a couple of weeks or a month or two. Otherwise, the colt's bones have closed and he is left with problems that will stay with him forever. Your farrier can only do so much. Trying to force "fix" a crooked-legged horse will often lead to more problems than leaving him balanced and natural will. You can stress bones and ligaments, trying to force them to do or be something they cannot do or be. Breeding a correct, straight-legged mare to a correct, straight-legged stallion is the best way to have a correct baby. Be sure that the colt is trimmed regularly and watch for any irregularities in the hoof growth.

Some colts will only need front shoes and can stay barefoot behind. Others will need a full set of four shoes, perhaps with a corrective measure such as a rolled or rocker toe, a squared toe,

A happy, responsive, well-trained horse is a joy to ride.

or a small trailer on a hind shoe. Your farrier has learned what he feels will best help your colt. As long as you are happy with your farrier's work, and he has a good reputation and a happy customer base, follow his directions.

Schedule a successive visit with the farrier during the current visit. That way, he can plan his schedule and will have the time to take care of your colt's feet. Calling three months from his last visit when your colt loses a shoe and expecting him to drop everything is unfair. You may find yourself looking for a new farrier. Pay him on time. He has a business to run and bills to pay, just as any other business does, and he and your vet may be the most vital people to have on your colt's side in case of an emergency.

*A horse that moves willingly to wherever you want with no
resentment is a pleasure to ride. Start your colts right,
talk to them in a language that they can understand,
and enjoy the time that you spend together.
(Here I am using my left leg to push him right.)*

Laurie Truskauskas grew up in Burlington, Connecticut, and started riding at the age of four. Numerous trips to the emergency room while learning to ride didn't dampen her enthusiasm, including the five days spent in the hospital after a crash while jumping a four-and-one-half-foot fence at a local fair where the rail was wired to the standard poles "to save the jump crew time."

Marriage at the age of fifteen, followed by the birth of twin boys on Christmas Eve, put the dream of learning to train horses on hold for a few years. Divorced five years later, she bought and owned a restaurant for ten years to support her family of twin boys and her horses. Learning that the only way to get what you want is to go out and get it, she went to work for Joe Ferro, one of the men responsible for starting the AQHA in 1942. Joe shared his knowledge of breeding and training top reining horses, filling in the holes that she had previously missed in her training education.

Going out on her own, she currently owns and trains at Silver Creek Farm in Athens, Texas. She starts colts for customers, retrains older horses, and gives lessons. A prior operation on her neck keeps her training schedule somewhat limited, yet it gave her the reason to pursue another dream: writing. They say to write what you know, and horses are what she knows. The first article that she wrote was bought by *Horse and Horseman* and featured as a center spread. That article, plus a second one, were part of a special pullout section on breeding, followed by a ten-part series on training. She has now published almost 100 articles and has almost completed a second book on training the Western horse.

Bob Porzio specializes in horse photography.

I N D E X